# You and I Eat the Same

# You and I Eat the Same

## On the Countless Ways Food and Cooking Connect Us to One Another

**Edited by Chris Ying**
**Foreword by René Redzepi**

ARTISAN | NEW YORK

Copyright © 2018 by MAD Foundation
Foreword © 2018 by René Redzepi
For photography credits, see page 215.

Managing editor: Aralyn Beaumont

Editor's Note: Early versions of different sections of the chapter "Culinary Difference Makes a Difference" have been published in *Saveur*, the *Huffington Post*, and *The Ethnic Restaurateur* (2016). This version has improved substantially under the guidance of and with the aid of edits by Stephanie Jolly.

Library of Congress Cataloging-in-Publication Data is on file.
ISBN 978-1-57965-840-3

Design by Hubert & Fischer

Artisan books are available at special discounts when purchased in bulk for premiums and sales promotions as well as for fund-raising or educational use. Special editions or book excerpts also can be created to specification. For details, contact the Special Sales Director at the address below, or send an e-mail to specialmarkets@workman.com.

For speaking engagements, contact speakersbureau@workman.com.

Published by Artisan
A division of Workman Publishing Co., Inc.
225 Varick Street
New York, NY 10014-4381
artisanbooks.com

Artisan is a registered trademark of Workman Publishing Co., Inc.
Published simultaneously in Canada by Thomas Allen & Son, Limited

Printed in China
First printing, September 2018

10 9 8 7 6 5 4 3 2 1

# Contents

# Foreword

For many years, Copenhagen was an island.

I don't mean that literally (although it's sort of true), but when it came to cuisine, for most of modern history, we were adrift from the rest of the world. As far as food was concerned, few people thought about Scandinavia.

But through a combination of perseverance and luck, the cooks in our small city managed to carve out a name for Nordic cuisine. In the past ten or fifteen years, people have begun to travel here from all around the world to eat at the great restaurants in town. I'm not mentioning this out of pride, but rather immense gratitude. The success of Copenhagen as a culinary destination has allowed us to connect with the rest of the world. Thank God, because things can be very insular here.

In 2011, we sought to solidify and grow that connection. In a muddy field on a small swath of land called Refshaleøen, we held our first MAD Symposium (*mad* is Danish for food). The word *symposium* makes it sound fancier than it was. In reality, we were just a few hundred people slogging through torrential rains to gather under a tent and talk about our world. Among us were people who grow food, cook food, study food, and write about food. We listened and learned from one another. We cooked and ate together. And at the end of the weekend, we decided we'd do it again the next year.

Since then, MAD has grown. We continue to host our annual gathering as well as smaller meetings for the local community here in Copenhagen. We've held conversations in New York and Sydney. We've awarded scholarships and grants, and shared the knowledge we've acquired freely and openly. In 2017, we launched a foraging initiative called VILD MAD that connects children and adults to wild foods in the world around them. In the years to come, we'll embark on an ambitious education initiative that will hopefully change the way young cooks and chefs learn and experience their trade.

What you hold in your hands, however, is perhaps the purest distillation of what MAD is about: connecting with one another. This book—the first in a series we're calling Dispatches—will hopefully reach a larger audience than MAD ever has before. More important, it carries a message that reminds me of those earlier days when we felt like we were on an island, searching for a link to the rest of the world. It turns out that good food is that link. You and I may not believe in the same things or share the same politics, but we can both appreciate a delicious meal. Food can't cure all the world's ails, but it's a start. If we can share a meal, maybe we can share a conversation, too.

—René Redzepi

# Introduction

There is plenty of evidence that you and I are different.

Our day-to-day experiences of the world tell us so on a nearly constant basis. You don't look or sound the same as me. And the odds of our political leanings, leisure-time preferences, and professional interests aligning exactly are close to nil. Perhaps you care about golf, whereas I do not care at all. I'm not a great singer—almost certainly worse than you. You and I don't eat the same things, either.

The differences between us are of immense value. Identity, personality, creativity, survival, love, conflict, and compromise stem from difference. Given that this book is about food, you can deduce that cuisine also benefits greatly from difference—different ingredients growing in different places, different socioeconomic conditions, different historical influences, different people cooking.

The bulk of literature about food tends to focus on educating readers about culinary difference. Browsing the cookbook aisles, one can find titles about the cooking of Japan, Germany, Greece, Morocco, Scandinavia, China, northern China, southern China, and the American South; the food of Mexico in general and the food of Oaxaca specifically; and how one's favorite local chef cooks potatoes and how a chef on the other side of the world does so.

In fact, there's a prevailing wisdom that says that when it comes to food, having good taste means being able to parse the world's various culinary traditions. The more minutiae you know about eating, the more impressive an eater you are. Being able to articulate the characteristics of Sichuan or Hunan cooking is cool. Expressing your disappointment in the quality of *mapo tofu* in America after a visit to Chengdu—even cooler. This is nothing new. Such expertise has been worn as a badge of credibility by young, hungry members of the middle class for more than a century. (Toward the end of this book, the historian Paul Freedman will tell you about how nineteenth-century bohemians were the ur-hipsters.)

Culinary difference can be a source of pride for cooks, too. This is well and good and important. People should derive dignity and distinction—not to mention entrepreneurial opportunity—from family recipes and traditions. (Later on you'll meet three women from San Francisco doing exactly that.) But it's easy to start believing that difference means everything, and that is a slippery slope. If we start thinking of difference as critical, we can start to imagine it as intrinsic. In other words, we might begin assuming that what we like to eat is immutable or hereditary, as are our values and our priorities. Our abilities. Our worth.

If you think I'm overstating the implications of dwelling on culinary difference, look at the myriad ways that food has been used to alienate us from one another: Kids teased about the contents of their lunches. Certain restaurants deemed "ethnic." African Americans portrayed in popular media as being unable to rise above their animalistic cravings for fried chicken. Chinese food seen as dirty and a source of mysterious illnesses.

Consider also the lengths we go to distinguish ourselves by what we eat. *I'm a foodie. I'm a vegan. I hate Korean food. I love Thai food. I don't eat fish. I won't eat bugs.* As a sort of extreme example, Mennonites have been on the move for centuries, trying to isolate themselves and their way of life from the rest of the world. For one of the chapters in this book, the excellent and worldly-wise writer Michael Snyder spent some time with a Mennonite community in rural Mexico. He was looking for a group of people who had managed to divest themselves fully from outside influence. Instead he found Mennonite farmers making and selling Mexican cheese, and sitting down to lunch with Mexican hot sauce and chilies on the table. The takeaway is that even if you commit your life to detaching from the rest of us, we'll eventually reach you—often through food.

This book is a catalog of such connections. Each chapter begins with a hypothesis. (Well, *hypothesis* implies more scientific method than we deserve credit for. Let's call it an observation.) Sesame is ubiquitous. Fire is the same wherever it burns. Everybody wraps meat in flatbread. If we've done our job properly, none of these should be especially taxing on your imagination. Scallion pancakes and tortillas are distinct forms, but you don't have to zoom out very far to see how similar they are in function.

Sometimes these connections are happenstance. Give humans a piece of meat and a piece of bread, and they're going to wrap the latter around the former, like clockwork. Other times, food appears connected because people have made it so. Curry, born in India, is a birthright of people in China, Japan, Thailand, Vietnam, South Africa, Jamaica, Portugal, England, and Scotland, among other places. It is by no means the same dish in all these various settings, but it remains identifiable and identified as curry. Curry follows the people who make and eat it, adapting and mutating as it moves.

You may sense an ulterior motive emerging. I won't be coy about it. Our thesis is this: Cuisine cannot exist without the free and fair movement of ingredients, ideas, and people. Deliciousness is an undeniable benefit of immigration. When people move around, food gets better. There are reasonable arguments to be made from wherever you stand on the politics of immigration, but the debate tends to go nowhere, because neither side is willing to admit to any kind of common ground. I'm inclined to think we'd do better to start the conversation with what we all stand to gain, and proceed from there.

I'm not trying to be didactic. This book is meant to be enjoyable to read. As you make your way through—and you should feel free to bounce around—hopefully you'll learn a few things, and also come across the occasional joke that makes you chuckle. A book, like food, is meant to entertain us even when it's trying to provoke.

A few paragraphs ago, I shied away from the word *hypothesis*. I'm going to invoke it again here to let you in on a little behind-the-scenes tidbit. This book's title, *You and I Eat the Same*, is a hypothesis. It was a placeholder I came up with before the contents were filled in, and proving its validity became a personal experiment. I wasn't sure how much truth there was to it when I wrote it. I'm still not prepared to say that you and I eat exactly the same. But after reading what our contributors had to say about the ways food links us together, I feel distinctly closer to other people. I hope when you're done reading this book, you'll feel the same.

—Chris Ying

# Everybody Wraps Meat in Flatbread

## Aralyn Beaumont

The cement is hot and the street is bustling. I do my best to stay out of the way as I reach out to pay the vendor, a man of few words and lightning-quick hands, who presents me with a wrapped bundle. Peeling open the paper reveals lightly charred meat tumbling out of a disk of warm, soft flatbread. I take a bite and keep walking.

You might be picturing this scene in Kolkata, with the vendor slinging *kati* rolls. Or maybe your mind went immediately to the dry, hot streets of Jerusalem and lamb shawarma. It's possible you imagined *rou jia mo*, the shredded-pork buns of Shaanxi Province in China. I could have been in my hometown of San Francisco, eating a carne asada taco. Any of these locations fit.

Wrapping meat in flatbread is a foundational practice of earth's cuisine. There are kebabs and tacos, which have broken free of their geographic contexts and become ubiquitous, but also beef-stuffed blinis, Peking duck wrapped in thin flour pancakes, and rye *flatkaka* with smoked lamb at Christmastime in Iceland. Anywhere you travel on earth, you'll find meat (or another staple protein) enveloped in starch, and people lining up for it.

It won't always come as a prewrapped package. We humans also like large pieces of flatbread served alongside curries, stews, soups, and platters of barbecued meats. Few things are more satisfying than tearing off a hunk of bread and using it to scoop meat and sop up the

Wherever humans roam the earth, we make flatbreads from the most commonly available grain.

13

A tortilla-wrapped burrito, prized for its portability and caloric density

juices. The phenomenon extends to vegetarian traditions, too, where meat may be swapped for legumes or protein-rich vegetables, but the breads remain.

Flatbreads can be baked, steamed, fried, or griddled. They vary in thickness from svelte crepe to puffy fry bread. They come in all shapes, shades, flavors, and sizes, and yet they all share the same essential role. Wherever there is grain, there is flatbread. It is usually a staple of the local citizenry, and someone has probably thought to wrap it around meat.

Certain flatbreads are omnipresent. Tacos can be found in nearly every city in America, whether at a taqueria, fast-food place, gas station, or fine-dining restaurant. Same with egg rolls. Kebabs feed drunk people everywhere. And where in the world has the convenient pita pocket not been exploited and filled?

The simple historical explanation for the ubiquity of meat wrapped in flatbread is that apart from stuffing meat directly into our mouths, wrapping it in a piece of bread is the most straightforward and cleanest way of eating with our hands. "Most people have always eaten most meals without cutlery, which remains true today," explains food historian Bee Wilson. "If you can create a dish that dispenses with the need for anything but fingers, you are winning."

Beef wrapped in a
scallion pancake, aka
*xian bing*

Humans have used flatbread to transfer meat into their mouths for at least a thousand years. The earliest recorded instance dates back to the first century BCE, when Rabbi Hillel the Elder wrapped lamb and bitter vegetables (horseradish with romaine leaves or endive) in matzo during Passover. Hillel's sandwich—still a tradition at Passover seders—grew from the prescription laid out in the book of Exodus instructing Jews to roast a sacrificed lamb and eat it with unleavened bread and bitter herbs in remembrance of the Israelites who fled Egypt ("They shall eat the flesh in that night, roast with fire, and unleavened bread; and with bitter herbs they shall eat it."—Exodus 12:8.) The herbs represent the bitterness of slavery, while the flatbread reflects the haste with which the Israelites had to flee Egypt, before the bread had time to rise. The sandwich derives its name, *korech*, from the Hebrew word *karech*, meaning "to encircle or surround."

Hillel created the *korech* ritual based on the Passover rules enumerated in Exodus, but it's probably safe to assume that he packaged all the components together because it was something he was already used to seeing. In other words, the meat-and-herb wrap is *at least* as old as Hillel, but, as Wilson points out in *Sandwich: A Global History*, in all likelihood, it was already being eaten in the Middle East before that.

While some of the lineage of flatbread-wrapped meat can be linked historically, what's enlightening is that much of it happened concurrently and separately. It seems hardwired into our nature: if we see a piece of bread and a piece of meat, we want to swaddle the latter in the former and put the whole thing in our mouths.

People have been consuming meat for three million years, ever since our early human ancestors started tenderizing it by pounding it with a mallet-like tool and eating it raw—long before the mastery of fire or cooking. When exactly we gained control of fire is a hotly contested issue—estimates range from two million to five hundred thousand years ago—but both fire and flatbread are inventions that sprung up independently in isolated areas at different periods throughout early human history.

The same is true of flatbreads, which may be the oldest baked good, predating oceanic travel, imperial conquest, colonialism, and other developments that led to the exchange of goods like pasta, tomatoes, spices, chilies, and chocolate. In fact, flatbreads came before ovens. The first ones were baked on the surface of hot stones or along the concave interior of fire pits.

The versatile *pide*, waiting to be deployed for any number of uses, including as a meat blanket

For breakfast in parts of China, we fill wheat and mung bean flatbreads (*jianbing*) with sausage, egg, scallions, and other accessories.

As a species, we humans find a way to make flatbread from whatever staple grain is around us: rye in Scandinavian crispbread; corn tortillas in Mexico and arepas in Venezuela; sorghum in Sudanese *kisra*; rice and lentils in Indian dosa. In Northern and Central Asia and parts of Africa, we bake wheat-based naan and *sangak* in tandoor ovens and use them to wrap up lamb. Farther north, where barley can withstand high altitudes and cold temperatures, we make *fatir* on upside-down woks. In Mali, millet-based *ngome* is topped with meat and vegetables; in Tunisia, semolina-based breads called *khobz tabouna* come out of tandoors.

Sometime between six thousand and three thousand years ago, teff became the staple crop of Ethiopia and was put to use in the spongy flatbread known as *injera*. Fermenting the teff batter generates air bubbles that burst and create hundreds of little craters in the finished bread. Once cooked, the *injera* is laid out like a tablecloth and topped with small servings of different mutton and vegetable stews and roasted cuts of beef called *tibs*. Anyone who's been to an Ethiopian restaurant will likely be familiar with *injera*, often made from a batter with buckwheat or sorghum incorporated into the mix.

In South Asia, rice flour is fermented with lentils for Indian dosas, which serve as a vehicle for lentil or potato masalas as well as lamb and chicken. In Vietnam, *bánh xèo* is made from a batter of rice flour and coconut milk and folded like an omelet around pork, shrimp, herbs, and bean sprouts. Vietnam's other flatbread, rice paper sheets known as *bánh tráng*, are steamed and used to wrap grilled pork, fish, meatballs, or skewered sausages like *nem nuong*.

Meanwhile, in Mesoamerica, the oldest grain is corn. People were using it to produce masa for tamale-like dishes thousands of years ago, but making a tortilla wasn't possible until around 700 BCE, when the process of nixtamalization entered the picture. Historians remain unsure how Aztec cooks first devised the ingenious process of soaking corn in an alkali (mineral lime) solution to break down the kernels

and thus allow them to cook faster, stay edible longer, and be more nutritious. But by 300 BCE, the tortilla was a prominent feature of Mesoamerican cuisine. In Oaxaca, farmers would wrap wild game in tortillas; elsewhere, the predominant filling was beans or squash. Spanish colonists in the sixteenth century would be the first to call them *tortillas*, which translates to "little cake"—a rather reductive name, in retrospect, for one of the most important culinary inventions in history.

The Spanish planted large fields of wheat and introduced livestock to the New World, which would eventually lead to the emergence of carne asada, goat *birria*, and pork carnitas tacos. *Al pastor* has its roots in the shawarma of Lebanon, which immigrants from the Middle East brought to the Yucatán in the late nineteenth century, as the Ottoman Empire began to fall apart. Vertically spit-roasted

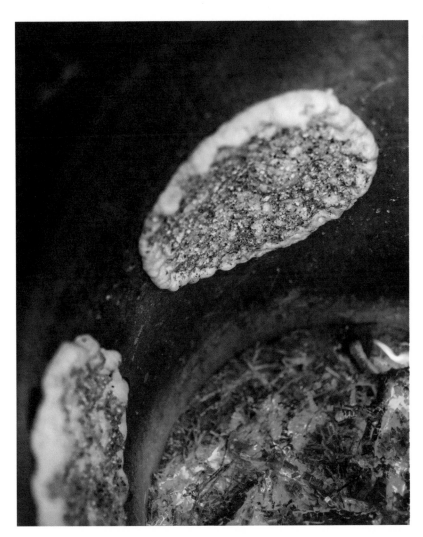

meat gradually made its way to central Mexico, where the lamb was swapped for chili-marinated pork. The flour tortilla emerged in the sixteenth century, and was eaten almost exclusively by European colonists until the nineteenth century, when some Mexican communities in the north began adopting it.

Native Americans farther north had a less symbiotic culinary experience with colonizers. Before Europeans arrived, the cuisine was defined by hyperlocal crops. The Cocopa and Yuma of the American Southwest ground mesquite beans into meal for flatbreads. Residents in the Northwest made flour from bunchgrass, while people in the south grew corn for a tortilla-like flatbread.

But in the nineteenth century, as tribes like the Navajo were stripped of their land and forced to move to reserves in New Mexico,

Corn tortillas: beloved by humans around the planet

it became impossible to introduce or sustain crops in the landscape. The American government distributed rations of flour, sugar, lard, and canned food. From these limited provisions, Native Americans created fry bread: a doughy flatbread made from refined white flour and fried in lard. (Today, restaurants in New Mexico and Arizona serve fry breads topped with ground beef and cheese as "Navajo tacos.")

In multiple senses, flatbread is a food of necessity. It arose from limited resources. It persists because something in our nature compels us to eat it.

A partial but fairly representative list of flatbreads from around the world, organized by their principal grain. Each of these is usually served alongside or wrapped around meat (or, in a few cases, protein-heavy vegetables). The places in parentheses indicate where you'll most likely find the bread in question, but as you now know, flatbread is everywhere. There is a lot of overlap and cross-pollination.

**Barley**
Fatir (Saudi Arabia)
Flatbrød (Norway)
Korkun (Tibet)

**Buckwheat**
Breton galette (France)

**Cassava**
Bammy (Jamaica)
Casabe (Dominican Republic)

**Corn**
Aish merahrah (Egypt)
Arepa (Venezuela)
Tortilla (Mexico)

**Millet**
Bajra roti, bajri bhakri, bajarichi bhakri (India)
Ngome (Mali)

**Oats**
Flatbrød (Norway)

**Potato**
Lefse and lompe (Norway)

**Rye**
Bolani (Afghanistan)
Flatkaka (Iceland)
Knekkebrød, knäckebröd, knækbrød, näkkileipä (Scandinavia)
Schuettelbrot (Austria)

**Rice**
Bánh cuon (Vietnam)
Bánh tráng (Vietnam)
Bánh xèo (Vietnam)
Cheong fun (Hong Kong)
Chokha ni rotli (India)
Dosa (India)

**Semolina**
Kesra (Algeria)
Msemen, malawi (North Africa)
Pane carasau (Sardinia)
R'ghayef (Morocco)

**Sorghum**
Jowar roti (India)
Kisra (Sudan)

**Teff**
Injera (Ethiopia, Eritrea, Somalia)

**Wheat**
Bai ji mo (China)
Balep (Tibet)
Barbari bread (Iran)
Blinis (Russia)
Chapati (India)
Chun bing (China)
Crepe (France)
Dhal puri (Trinidad and Tobago)
Ekmek (Turkey)
Fry bake (Trinidad and Tobago)
Fry bread (United States)
Gözleme (Turkey)
Jianbing (Taiwan)
Khachapuri (Georgia)
Khubz (Iraq)
Lahmacun (Turkey)
Lahoh (North Africa)
Lao bing (China)
Lavash, lavosh, lawaash (Middle East)
Murtabak (Malaysia)
Naan (Central Asia and India)
Nan-i-Afghani (Afghanistan)
Nang (China)
Pancakes (United States)
Paratha (India)
Piadina (Italy)
Pide (Turkey)
Pita (Mediterranean and Middle East)
Popiah, lumpia (Southeast Asia)
Roti canai (Malaysia)
Rumali roti (India)
Sabaayad (Somalia)
Sangak (Iran)
Shao bing (China)
Sheermal (India)
Tandoori roti (India)
Trapizzino (Italy)
Tunnbröd (Sweden)
Xian bing (China)
Yufka (Turkey)

# Much Depends on How You Hold Your Fork

## Wendell Steavenson

I was invited for lunch. My hosts worried if it was too cold to eat on the terrace, but I said their view of the foothills of the Pyrenees was too beautiful to resist. The wish of the guest was deferred to; an extra sweater was fetched. Then I worried about using my fingers to pry the flesh from the bones of my fried whole sea bream. My concern grew so great that my conversation faltered and I stopped to explain, "I am very aware of my table manners, eating with the woman who wrote the book on them!"

My hosts both laughed.

"Oh, we are very informal here!" reassured Dr. Margaret Visser, renowned cultural anthropologist and author of *The Rituals of Dinner: The Origins, Evolution, Eccentricities, and Meaning of Table Manners*, first published in 1991 and still the definitive work on why we hold our forks and knives the way we do and what this tells us about ourselves and society.

We drank white wine with the fish. Afterward there was a perfect gooey *Époisses* cheese, and Margaret's husband, Colin, opened a bottle of red to go with it. Colin and Margaret, both originally from South Africa, settled in Canada, where they raised two children and were university professors in Toronto, and now, in their retirement, divide their time between an apartment in Toulouse and the big old country farmhouse where I met them, which they bought more than forty years ago. I am British American and live in Paris. Inevitably the conversation turned, as it often does among expats, to the peculiar social habits of our host nation. The French insistence on greeting a shopkeeper properly by saying "Bonjour" before any transaction can be made, the way a regular patron at a restaurant will shake hands with the maître d' when he arrives, the proper methods to cut different cheeses, the designated progression of alcohol over an evening—from sweet aperitif to wine with dinner to brandied digestif.

"Food is never just something to eat," Visser has argued for thirty years. As she writes in *The Rituals of Dinner*, "We use eating as a medium for social relationships: satisfaction of the most individual of needs becomes a means of creating community." From family and fealty, feudalism to federalism, food is communication, communion; it defines status and relationships; it is politics.

Margaret Visser's father was a mining engineer. She grew up in a copper-mining town in Zambia in the forties and fifties. "A colonial backwater," as she described it to me. "We ate the most abominable food imaginable. My parents belonged to the colonial generation, who believed food was beneath contempt." This meant a diet of canned sausage, sandwich spread, condensed milk. When the situation arose, her father, "a pure Edwardian," would stand to carve a roast, sharpening the knife as dramatically as if it were a sword (harkening back, as Visser later discovered in her research, to the days when the nobility regarded carving meat as an essential social skill). Her mother's only dish was roast potatoes. Meals were cooked by Nanny, a local woman rendering a European cuisine that she herself did not eat.

Margaret's father was full of stories, and when she was six, he told her one about three children served soup that was too hot to eat. The children's father asked each one what they would do. The first boy answered that he would blow on the soup, the second boy that he would stir it until it became cool. The little girl, however—the heroine of the tale—replied that she would put down her spoon and wait for a little while until the soup cooled. Margaret remembers very clearly being confounded by this parable. "I thought, 'This does not make any sense. What's wrong with blowing on soup? Why is the right thing to do to wait a little while?' That question," she says, "is where my books came from."

Europeans eat sitting at a table. As a child, Visser often visited Nanny in her home, where they sat on the floor (as most families in most cultures do) and shared from one large bowl. What difference

Eating together is a fundamental human activity.

does it make? Visser smiled when I asked this. "When people sit on the floor, they eat from a communal dish," she explained. "At a table, people are separated, each has their own plate. One is a group, the other is individual."

Visser taught Homer and Greek to university students for eighteen years before she began to examine quotidian tropes and traditions in regular radio discussions and in a magazine column entitled "The Way We Are," which delved into the hinterlands of everything from Santa Claus to avocados, high heels, tipping, and spoonerisms. "I was trying to find a line; there were things I wanted to say about why human beings behave in the way that they do." Food and the essential everyday experience of eating seemed a good vehicle to use.

Her first book, *Much Depends on Dinner*, published in 1986, took a simple menu and investigated the histories, modern iterations, and social implications of its ingredients. She described the evolution of corn from an indigenous American staple to a ubiquitous industrial behemoth, and questioned the ethics of cheap chicken at a time when the miseries of farming in battery cages were largely unknown.

The book's success—it was a bestseller, garnering prizes in the United States and Britain—was a surprise, and it laid the foundation for a new way of writing, not only about food, but about history and the human experience itself. Visser told me that she was pleased to see that potatoes, cod, and salt were now being given their own biographies. "Finding the ordinary interesting is a modern and bloody

Three women share a communal hot pot.

Following spread: Two women share a communal hot pot.

good idea ... it's a kind of democracy, an egalitarianism. It's we, the ordinary people, saying we are interesting, too, not just the kings and warriors."

In her next book, *The Rituals of Dinner*, she set out to examine how we eat. The book hopscotches from Amazonian tribes to Victorian dining rooms, biblical references, and the aisles of American supermarkets, comparing and contrasting myriad mores, habits, customs, traditions, and taboos. Visser traces the evolution of knives and forks and chopsticks and asks: What is the point of a fork (something I have often wondered), and why do they have four prongs? Why is it rude in Japan to stick your chopsticks into your rice? Why do Westerners have a sweet dessert at the end of the meal while the Chinese conclude with soup?

Some things can be explained as technological developments— bread trenchers giving way to ceramic plates, for instance. Others are fashion: the tradition of an appetizer followed by a main course and then dessert was popularized by a Russian diplomat in Paris in the eighteenth century; before this, at European grand banquets, dishes were laid out on the table all at once for diners to serve themselves. Some habits were designed for safety: knives are weapons—pass them handle first. The fork evolved from spikes used to hold meat for carving; they were popularized in Italy and Spain during the late Middle Ages as a way to eat meat without getting one's fingers greasy. But detractors have complained through the centuries that they are a useless implement for ferrying peas or beans into the mouth.

Table manners illustrate and codify complex social interchanges. Visser follows millennia of gender politics that echo from the ancient men-only Greek symposia to the habit of English ladies removing themselves from the dining room so that the men could relax with their port and cigars to the traditions in many African cultures of a wife eating only after her husband has been fed the choicest morsels.

Differences in what's considered genteel are legion and contradictory. In some places, it is polite to eat with gusto; in others, a guest should demur and pretend he is not hungry. A fart is one society's compliment, another's faux pas. Spitting and smoking used to be perfectly acceptable in European company; no longer. So far as I can tell, there is no common thread of perceived politeness that unites peoples separated by time or geography. In Kurdistan, I once attended a lunch at a sheik's house, during which everyone ate in silence and stood up as quickly as possible when leaving so that someone else could take their place. In the mountains of Georgia, I ate with a poor village family who practically held me hostage with an endless series of toasts that I was honor bound to drink to. I remembered my confusion and awkwardness during these experiences. I had always imagined that coming together to eat, breaking bread together, represented a universal social custom. *Do we humans have a shared humanity?* I wondered as I read a chapter on cannibalism.

When I asked Visser for a unifying theme that ran through the world's table manners, she shook her head: "Disgust is learned, not inherent." Regulations and rituals represented "universalities only in the abstract." It doesn't matter what the rules are, only that there are rules and that they are agreed upon and that breaking them tends to cause ostracism and such social distress that they rarely are. Cannibalism in the Aztec Empire, Visser writes in *The Rituals of Dinner*, was a regular and accepted practice, but at the same time, it was highly

ritualized, "no more lacking in table manners than is any other kind of meal."

I pressed Visser for instances she had witnessed of bad manners. She thought for a moment and said she had a friend who chewed with her mouth open and who could not understand why she had so few invitations to dinner. I thought about my own experiences of eating in many different countries and cultures. I have seen riots and fights and defenseless people being beaten, listened to deriding and discrimi-

nating opinions; I've been robbed and sexually harassed. But I could not think of a single instance of witnessing someone behaving really badly while eating—grabbing food, burping, shoveling food into their mouth with their hands, yelling for more. Eating etiquette is apparently more strongly ingrained than religion or morality.

"Not conforming can result in a pitiless rejection of the person,"Visser says. "It matters terribly." Manners are not consistent, but Visser rejects the idea that they are completely arbitrary. Having dug into their origins, their uses, their reasons, she believes, "The universal is the sharing of food, and that is the idea of justice." Rules mean that mealtimes are not fights over food. "Because you have to eat every day, it's too difficult to have a free-for-all every time you sit down to a meal."

It is tempting to assume that manners engender social cohesion and harmony, but Visser shook her head at my mention of this. Behavior codes can be used to exclude as much as to include. Between host and guest there is a delicate balance of power—giving and receiving, responsibility and obligation. Visser argues that at the core of all rituals, there is a basic threat of violence that must be overcome by signs and signals.

I had been invited to stay the night. Colin made meatballs and a Spanish tortilla for dinner. Trying to be a good guest, I washed up afterward, expressly aware of the reciprocity that I had been taught was polite. The next day I woke with more questions than I had begun with. I realized that more important than understanding the point of a fork was the act of questioning its existence. At the heart of Visser's work is an extraordinary and original curiosity. Since her groundbreaking study of food and society, she has written books on gratitude, fate, and architecture. Nothing in her world is taken for granted. "I refuse to accept the ordinary as dull. Common things—it stands to reason—are the most important things, the ones with history and politics and meaning, the ones with clout."

"Are we what we eat or how we eat?" I asked her finally, as Colin cooked a tagine for lunch. In *Much Depends on Dinner*, Visser describes how the large amount of labor required to cultivate rice gave rise to a social culture that emphasized the collective over the individual.

Does our increasing reliance on monocultures mirror the globalization that may be erasing cultural gaps? In the West, dining rooms have gone the way of the dodo. People often eat alone, and in front the TV. There is an epidemic of obesity. Visser sees a correlation.

"Consumerism comes from the verb *to consume*. It's a food metaphor. We now have an economic system that is allied to food and eating." Cheap processed food is carefully designed to deliver a bliss point of moreishness. "I believe it's engineered so that the one percent can have ninety percent of the money," Visser says. "The multitudes are quiet. They don't understand why they are fat or sad or need to go shopping to feel better."

Dining rituals stand in for values. As such, they are constantly changing. In our lifetime, we have seen the rise of an informality (me eating fish with my fingers) that would have been disquieting to our parents' or grandparents' generation. Maybe, Visser posits, this could represent a reaction to the fragmentation and the loosening of family ties. Formality, after all, is about creating distance; informality, she says—hearteningly—might be about wanting to come together again.

"But," she counters, never one to allow an easy answer, "now it is considered rude to be formal. It's only the opposite to what we had before. So it is the same. All you have done is tick instead of tock."

Manners, even in their absence, are inescapable.

# Mennonite Cheese Is Mexican Cheese

## Michael Snyder

It is seven a.m. in the Mennonite colonies dead in the center of the northern Mexican state of Durango. In the Mexican settlement across the highway, where they observe daylight saving, it's already eight, but nothing will open for another two hours. Here in the Mennonite colonies, it's a different world: the morning still starts with the sun and work stops for no one but God.

Abraham Klassen began his day at five a.m. colony time, milking his eighteen cows, then sitting down with his wife, three children, and in-laws for a silent prayer and breakfast of instant coffee and homemade bread spread with homemade butter and homemade jam. Just before seven, he hitched a rickety wooden cart to the back of his brother-in-law's faded orange tractor and went out to collect milk from the neighbors.

The night before, giant storm clouds walked in on tall stilts of rain, leaving the oat fields drenched. Low stalks of corn, just a few weeks into their summer flush, were neck deep in standing water; the rutted dirt roads, cut with Teutonic rectitude past white fences and white churches, were totally waterlogged.

"Days like today, it's too muddy to work in the fields," Klassen tells me in Spanish as he hefts steaming metal canisters onto the cart. He squints up at the clouds, rolling in like gauze to bandage the huge frontier sky. "There's always something to do. You get a break from one thing, it's just a chance to do another."

Dairy farmer Abraham Klassen in Durango, Mexico

Klassen's family emigrated from Canada to Durango in 1924, two years after the first Mexican Mennonite colonies were founded in the neighboring state of Chihuahua. A third-generation resident here, his accent is pure *norteño*—fast and wry, as though everything's a joke if you just pay attention—yet still oddly clipped with the precise diction of his mother tongue, Plattdeutsch, or Low German.

Klassen and his brother-in-law Abraham Wall are among a dozen teams of milk collectors who traverse the thirty-four Mennonite colonies—spread over 22,000 hectares—each morning and each evening. Together they gather literal tons of milk to take to the Quesería Holanda, by far the largest business in the valley.

Founded by Mennonites in 1970, Holanda has operated as a cooperative since 1993. Earnings are distributed among members, including milk providers, milk deliverers, and the landless young people who turn the milk into cheese at the company's factory. Today, 80 percent of all milk produced by Durango's eight thousand Mennonites goes to Holanda's plant, a total of about 32,000 tons a year processed into 3,200 tons of cheese (two smaller plants and a fair number of home producers use much of the rest). That's an average of 100 tons of milk collected each working day, a startling amount for a community that barely used electricity until twenty years ago and didn't have cars until ten years after that.

Old Colony Mennonites, as the most conservative sect of the Mennonite faith are known, live a deliberately anachronistic life in order to fulfill their radical interpretation of Christ's command to live simply. That means eschewing modern technologies like TV and the Internet and, for the super conservative, even cars and electricity. Most of all, it means remaining free from the influences of the outside world. In Durango, dairy made that dream possible.

With the income from the *quesería*, the community funds its own German-language schools, maintains its own roads, and builds its own wells. They adjudicate their own internal disputes and make their own decisions about which innovations from the outside world enter the community and when. Salaries for teachers and the community's governors—elected every two years by the community's adult men—are calculated according to the value of milk.

The first person I met when I arrived in Durango was Isaac Enns, the director of the Quesería Holanda. We sat in the distribution office, a dim white box of a room overlooking the Plaza de Armas in Nuevo Ideal—"New Ideal"—the Mexican town that provides the

Mennonite colonies with everything they can't produce themselves, from coffee and flour to cell phones and lawyers. Dressed in the Old Colony Mennonite uniform of black overalls, plaid shirt, and broad-brimmed cowboy hat, Enns looked incongruously formal with his arms crossed over a long desk neatly piled with orders and invoices. He smiled affably and spoke candidly, his deeply creased face occasionally shattered by a sudden, boyish grin.

"I heard a saying recently," he said near the end of our conversation. "It was in German, of course, but it said, 'The best thing you can give your children is what your father gave to you. If you don't, then the soul dies.'" He paused, as though considering the veracity of the statement, then, deciding in its favor, added, "Our traditions are what keep us alive."

In the fields the next morning, the cornstalks dazzle under a sheen of fresh rain and puddles reflect the low, ragged mountains circling the valley like a fortress. Klassen is loading the last of the milk onto the cart—some ninety canisters, more than 2,500 liters. I ask what he dreamed of doing when he was a kid. He smiles, his brilliant blue eyes quizzical, as though it were the most eccentric question he's ever heard, but he answers without hesitation: "What I'm doing now."

———

Nuevo Ideal looks like just about any other small town in northern
Mexico. It's dusty, flat, and hectic. Blocky facades, once painted in
brilliant shades of fuchsia or turquoise, have been worn gray by years
of hard sun, hard wind, and the occasional scouring rain. Restaurants
with names like Twins and Montana sell two-foot-long *burritos gigantes*
and steaming bowls of menudo. Big families gather in the leafy main
square on weekday afternoons to lounge in a scant patch of shade—
except on days when the local toughs, under the control of a shadowy
figure known as El Talibán, turn up to brandish their guns and remind
everyone who's boss.

Before it was incorporated as a municipality, Nuevo Ideal was
a small rural settlement called Los Patos, named for the thousands

of ducks (*patos*) that used to fly down from Canada to winter in the shallow wetland lagoons that dotted the valley. Incorporated in 1989, the modern town owes its existence to another Canadian migration, when the first Mennonite settlers arrived on six trains from Saskatchewan on June 15, 1924.

Isaac Enns's great-grandfather was among those first Mennonite settlers in Los Patos and left behind a diary, rendered in the elaborate gothic script used to write Plattdeutsch. "They packed everything they owned. Their clothes, furniture, pots and pans," Enns tells me on the day we meet. "They even brought their horses, chickens, and cows." Everything they would need to sustain a life in isolation.

Mennonites have been on the move since their sect's founding in northern Germany in the sixteenth century as part of the Protestant Reformation. Over the next three centuries, their migrations took them through Holland, Poland, Siberia, and modern-day Ukraine, always in search of the same basic conditions: open land to cultivate; governments that would grant them exemptions from military service (Mennonites are pacifists); freedom of religious expression (including the once controversial practice of adult baptism); and freedom to educate their children as they saw fit.

Mennonites typically say they aim to "be in the world but not of the world," an interpretation of a phrase from the Gospel according to John. To do that, they created a closed society aloof from politics and power and, beginning in the twentieth century, from modernity itself. If most immigrants leave home in search of a better future, then Old Colony Mennonites emigrate in search of a freer past.

The Mennonites first learned to live in closed communities in Germany as a necessary protection against the persecutions of the Reformation. In Switzerland, they learned to drain marshlands and make cheese. In 1562, a wealthy Polish family invited them to settle in the wetlands around the Vistula River outside Danzig (later Weimar, now Gdańsk). When Prussia took the region in the late eighteenth century, the Lutheran church forced the government to restrict land acquisitions for other religious groups, particularly the Mennonites, who had expanded their land holdings and transformed the swampy Vistula into productive agricultural terrain. Nowhere were the Mennonites considered citizens.

In 1762, Catherine the Great issued a mandate to encourage foreign immigration into Russia's vast hinterlands. The Mennonites heeded her call and founded their first settlement in the Crimea in

1789, with the understanding that they would not preach their faith to Russians. As they had in Danzig, the Russian Mennonite population grew quickly. They planted wheat and were well-off, relative to the Russian peasants who worked as their farmhands. In order to provide each new generation with land, they founded hundreds of daughter colonies, spreading south into the Caucasus and east through Samara, Siberia, and Manchuria.

In 1870, Czar Alexander II eliminated the military exemption granted by his great-grandmother. That year, a third of Russia's fifty thousand Mennonites fled to North America, many with nothing more than what they could carry, where the American Homestead Act and Canada's Dominion Lands Act had opened the great central prairies to western colonization (at the expense, of course, of North America's indigenous peoples). About seven thousand of the most conservative Mennonites went to Canada, where more lenient rules made it easier to replicate the world they'd left behind in Russia. This is when they started identifying themselves by the term *Altkolonier*, or Old Colony.

When the Canadian government made English-medium education compulsory in 1918, the most conservative Mennonites, mostly in Manitoba and Saskatchewan, decided to move yet again. A year later, they sent a small delegation in search of a new homeland in Latin America, where several countries had also opened their borders to European immigrants in an attempt to populate—and whiten—their interiors. Enns's great-grandfather was on that delegation, too, and traveled through Argentina, Paraguay, Uruguay, and Brazil looking for arable land and accommodating governments.

When one of the delegates died in Brazil, the Mennonites cut their journey short. On the ship from Buenos Aires to New York, the Mexican Consul in Buenos Aires noticed the peculiar-looking group—all blond, all blue-eyed, wearing farmer's clothes from another era—and asked why they were so despondent. "They explained that they had to leave Canada or they would never be able to maintain their traditions," Enns says. "And he said, 'What you're looking for, you might find in Mexico.'" Within three years, the Mennonites had bought land and founded a settlement in Chihuahua. Two years later, the trains arrived in Durango.

Enns's great-grandfather wrote about the droughts and frosts that killed off the first crops of wheat. Forage crops like oats, sorghum, and corn stood up better to Durango's high-altitude climate. So when the wheat failed, the community turned to their cows. They produced milk, cream, butter, and cheese; took it to the roadside in their horses and buggies; and sold it to anyone coming or going from Durango, the eponymous state capital, then a sleepy frontier town seventy-five miles to the south.

Modernity crept in slowly. First with rubber tires for tractors, then with electricity for industrial uses, then with pumps for wells. Changes were introduced through voting, open only to men. Those who modernized early were excommunicated and, in many cases, formed new congregations aligned with more liberal branches of the Mennonite church. Today there are eleven churches represented in the colonies, which the Old Colony Mennonites call "different religions."

In 1999, the introduction of electricity into Mennonite homes created what the Durango-based historian Liliana Salomón Meraz describes as "the Schism." Within a year, all ten of the community's religious leaders moved to Argentina, leaving the community without pastors for months. A few years later, Mennonite families started buying trucks; now most households have two or three.

But food began changing long before electricity or trucks came in. As Mennonite dairy products came to dominate the local market ("cheese" and "Mennonite" are pretty much synonymous in northern Mexico), Mexican food started turning up in Mennonite homes. The first generation, Enns tells me, "spent years making biscuits out of ground corn and baking them in the oven, and they would come out rock hard. They would stand around chewing when everyone else was making tortillas." Now most households in the colonies eat tortillas and frijoles several times a week. For special occasions they go to town for burritos and gorditas.

On the other hand, when Mexicans in Nuevo Ideal want a nice meal, they cross the highway to the restaurant at the Hotel Fiesta, run by a family of liberal Mennonite Brethren who dress in modern clothes and speak fluent Spanish. Their most popular dish is pizza, topped with a slick white blanket of perfectly melted, slightly sour *queso menonita*.

One morning, I visited the home of Johann and Sarah Harder, relatives of Abraham Klassen, to taste some traditional Mennonite cooking. At eleven a.m., Sarah was already hard at work in the expansive kitchen of her modest rancher, rolling out triangles of wheat dough to stuff with salted milk curds for a pierogi-like dish called *wareniki*. Sunshine filtered through a picture window, as though God were her personal director of photography. Her daughters, Ana and

Aganeta, moved efficiently between a gas stove, where they tended to a boiling pot of homemade pork sausage (which they referred to as chorizo), and a room-sized pantry where Sarah keeps dozens of mason jars stuffed with preserved beets, sauerkraut, apricot marmalade, and pickled pineapple.

At the table, we prayed and, in silence, ate a spread straight out of eighteenth-century Russia. We smashed fresh cream into boiled potatoes and drizzled it over the *wareniki*, their curd fillings mildly salty and sour, their skins thick and chewy. There were homemade pickles, racy with vinegar; baskets of homemade bread, the first thing Sarah learned to make as a twelve-year-old; and slices of *salchichón*, a smoked beef and garlic sausage made by a few families in the colonies that tastes, more than anything, like a very good kosher hot dog. Next to a tub of hand-churned butter were a bottle of Valentina hot sauce and a nearly empty can of pickled jalapeños.

The colony hasn't grown its territory since the 1940s, when it purchased the last of its 22,000 hectares from the government. But families haven't stopped growing. Most of the employees at the *quesería* are young men without property. Roughly 10 percent of the Mennonite population travels north each year to work alongside other Mexicans as migrant laborers on Canadian farms. Some have moved to Canada permanently. More conservative families, disappointed in the introductions of electricity and cars, have bought land in newer colonies in the states of Zacatecas, Campeche, and Quintana Roo, or moved farther still to Paraguay, Bolivia, and Argentina.

Anna Becker, now twenty-nine, left Durango with her parents at the age of four, returning to Mexico each winter until moving back permanently nine years ago to marry. Becker works weekdays at the Integrated Mennonite Services (Servicios Integrales Menonitas, or SIM) office, where she helps organize Spanish classes for the community's adult women; sells Bibles in German, English, and Spanish; and lends out Christian books, Christian music, and Christian movies to anyone interested.

When I first enter the SIM office, Anna and I speak in Spanish. It only takes a moment for her to ask if I speak English. When I say yes, she heaves a sigh of relief. "I'm trying to learn, but my Spanish is terrible," she says. As an outsider, Anna is keenly aware of the local system's shortcomings. Children here attend schools for four hours each day, six months each year, from ages six to twelve (eleven for girls). Their textbook is the Bible, written in High German. Immediately after finishing school, they start to work. Young men will often learn Spanish working in local workshops or from fellow farmhands. Few women learn the language, a frustration Anna feels herself.

"I don't think there would be anything wrong with giving kids here a better education," Anna says. "Agriculture can't last forever, so the next generation is going to *have* to do other kinds of work, and to do anything else here you need to speak Spanish."

She gives a timid smile. "Unfortunately, I'm not the one to make that decision." Anna asks my photographer, Felipe, about his camera and his work. She's always dreamed of being a photographer, she says. "It's so nice to go back and look at stories from your community. Lots of people around here—they just don't know their own history." But going back to school to learn "isn't really an option."

For Anna, technologies like digital photography are an indisputable good; the Internet—still technically prohibited, though its use is increasingly common among young people—is both indispensable and irresistible. It's how she stays connected to her family in Canada, and it's allowed her husband to manage his own business, a mechanic's shop near the entrance to the colonies. The *quesería* started using computers years ago to manage its accounts, just as it started using electricity to process its cheeses long before electricity came to private homes. The same institution that allows the community to maintain its separate world is also the wedge in the door for new technologies.

Since the Schism, it's also become increasingly clear what little the old traditions can do to isolate the community from the harsh realities of life in modern Mexico. From 2009 to 2013, a spate of drug war–related kidnappings hit Nuevo Ideal and bled quietly into the colonies. Liliana Salomón Meraz, who was deeply embedded with the community during those years, tells me, "People were being kidnapped and the community had no choice but to cooperate. They were afraid, just like the rest of us." In Chihuahua, where violence and water shortages are far bigger problems, some families have started escaping—to Russia.

Peter Braun, elected as bishop the year after the Schism, tells me that several Durango Mennonites were arrested on drug trafficking charges in those years. By far the most conservative person I met in Durango, Braun looks a solid decade older than his sixty-two years. His eyes and face are the same raw shade of red; his bald pate, hidden most of the time under a cowboy hat, is several shades lighter, like an arm just out of a cast. Walking into his dimly lit home, we pass through two large kitchens where tables are spread with freshly baked cookies, each topped with a cloud of gelatin-whipped egg white— another signature Mennonite product. His wife nods to us as we walk by, methodically spreading each cookie with a layer of chocolate.

Braun sees those incarcerations as a failure of tradition. "They're where they belong," he says sternly of the convicts as the sun begins to sink beyond the limp, lacy curtains, "because they didn't want to do the work they were meant to do."

Durango is not my first exposure to Anabaptist groups in the Americas. I grew up in suburban Baltimore, and on a few occasions, my family made trips to Pennsylvania's Lancaster County to visit Amish Country and Hersheypark. I remember horses and buggies and rustic wooden furniture. We would stay at a place called the Red Caboose Motel (it's still there), where the rooms are nested, as the name suggests, in retrofitted red train cabooses, which made those short trips feel like journeys.

In 2011, while living in Chile, I visited the Paraguayan Gran Chaco, the vast, dry forest that the Spanish once knew as the *infierno verde*—"green hell"—which covers the whole of western Paraguay and extends into Bolivia and Argentina. Mennonites first arrived there in the early 1920s, first in a wave from Canada, then in a second wave at the end of the decade when many fled Russia after the Bolshevik Revolution. They've since transformed the Chaco into one of Paraguay's most economically advanced regions. The Chaco Mennonites see themselves as having taken "empty" land and made it fruitful. To do that, they've deforested huge swaths of the largest contiguous ecosystem in South America outside the Amazon, and driven as many as nine aboriginal groups out of isolation and into lives of manual labor on Mennonite cattle ranches. In Filadelfia, the main Mennonite settlement in the Chaco, malarial shanties encircle the tidy town center like a rash, a *Twilight Zone* mash-up of the modern Midwest and the Reconstruction-era South. I remember one afternoon seeing an indigenous woman and her children, all dressed in rags, selling watermelons from a wheelbarrow near the giant silos of the peanut factory as shiny white pickups rolled silently by. The Chaco Mennonites are both in *and* of the world.

Later that year, I visited a family of American Amish who'd moved to southern Bolivia in the nineties. They spent nearly a decade among the Old Colony Mennonites before looking for a new home even farther afield. They found a patch of land abutting Madidi National Park deep in the northern rain forests, where they built a log cabin straight out of the nineteenth century, save for the solar panel powering its single electric bulb. A waterwheel turns the mill where the family patriarch, born in Kentucky, makes furniture for sale. They grow their own cacao; one night during my stay, the eldest daughter, Judith, turned the beans into a perfect slab of chocolate cake soaked in a warm bath of fresh milk. For a treat, the youngest boys, towheaded Nelly and his adopted brother, Kaiko, squeezed hot, frothy milk straight from the cow's udder into a metal jug slick with homemade cane syrup. Buttery, grassy, and bittersweet with the molasses-like syrup, it is among the best things I've ever tasted. One afternoon, Nelly greeted me with a hen in one hand and an ax in the other and asked me if I wanted to kill the hen. That night, we had chicken soup for dinner.

The Mennonites of Durango live between these two worlds, coexisting with their non-Mennonite neighbors while maintaining a cautious distance. In conversations with residents of Nuevo Ideal, I hear the Mennonites described variously as "hardworking," "efficient," "dedicated," and "perfect." They are also, without exception, described as outsiders.

Angelica Debora, a chemist from Durango, is one of three non-Mennonite employees at the *quesería*, and the only non-Mennonite who works at the factory. "Everyone dresses the same, so for a long time I thought they all looked the same," she tells me one morning while testing samples of milk for antibiotics. Over the years, she's made friends with some of the guys who work there, including Abraham Klassen, who jokes with her playfully: "They told me that when they go to shop at Sam's Club in Durango, they all share the same membership card. I think for most Mexicans, they all look the same."

However distant their cultures may remain, the Mexican and Mennonite communities in Nuevo Ideal are also mutually dependent. Mexican ranchers occasionally contribute milk to the *quesería* or work as farmhands on Mennonite land. They bring their cars to Mennonite mechanics, buy the trimmings of Mennonite cheese to make quesadillas and *chiles rellenos*, and make up the majority of the clientele at Mennonite fast-food joints like the Lonchería Menonita on Nuevo Ideal's main drag.

Inside the restaurant, a big banner menu in red and yellow hangs over the counter and open kitchen, where Mexican employees assemble hulking sandwiches entirely from products sourced across the highway. Everything from the burger patties to the cheese to the rolls is made by members of the owner's family.

Isaac Heide, thirty-three, opened the *lonchería* two years ago. His family had just come back from a year and a half of living in Canada, where they'd moved after one of his eighteen siblings was kidnapped during Mexico's crime wave. Heide also spent the first seven years of his life in Canada. When the family came back in 1991, Isaac's father decided to buy a car; he was excommunicated in short order. The entire extended family is now part of the evangelically inclined Mennonite Brethren church.

Isaac's plan is to turn the *lonchería* into a regional, and eventually national, franchise. Just last year he patented the name of the restaurant, sparking a small controversy. "People asked, 'How can you do that?' And I explained, 'I'm not saying you can't use the name *here*, but I want to *grow*.'"

Mornings at the Hotel Fiesta tend to be busy. Most of the rooms are occupied by big Mennonite families down from Canada to visit their relatives in the new old country. The hotel, which is really a motel, sits on Mexican-owned land on the Mennonite side of the highway. It's impeccably clean and shockingly cheap, a perfect wedge of banal Americana between Mexico and the Mennonites.

Doors of hotel rooms and pickup trucks start opening and closing at six a.m. At nine, the parking lot is teeming with kids dressed in plaid shirts and baseball caps or long dresses and white bonnets. Around midday, a pair of young blond women in long-sleeved floral dresses and white sneakers appears with metal cleaning carts, dipping into rooms to make beds and replace dirty towels. Mexican families from across the highway stream in and out of the restaurant, which, on most days, is managed by the owners' ultra-efficient eldest daughter, Cassandra.

One morning, I meet a man called Abraham Goertzen, visiting from Ontario with two of his five kids. Goertzen moved from Durango to Canada fifteen years ago at the age of twenty-eight. At the time, he tells me, he was working at the Quesería Holanda, earning 75 pesos per day. "I had to work five days just to buy a sack of flour," he tells me in English, his third language, German diction nipping at the ankles of his loping Canadian vowels. "Like I say, money talks these days, and there's just more work up there." In Durango, he tells me, "Mennonites don't really mix with the Mexicans, but in Canada, both of my neighbors are English. Where I live, you wouldn't know where the Mennonite community begins."

A few years back, Goertzen built himself equipment to make nonpasteurized *queso menonita*, just like his mother and mother-in-law used to make, which he sells to members of the community. I ask how many Mexican Mennonites live around him. He answers in figures: "Well, I started out with two hundred liters of milk per week"—about twenty blocks of cheese—"and now I make fifteen hundred, and it's almost not enough."

Goertzen tells me he was nervous that he might run into trouble with immigration authorities on the trip down: "I was *sure* people would see that I'm a Mexican." Goertzen is six feet tall with ruddy cheeks and fair skin—not, I told him, the profile that most Americans associate with Mexico. He shrugs. "I *am* Mexican."

If, as Enns told me, tradition is what keeps the community alive, then after five hundred years on the move, migration itself may be the most important Mennonite tradition of all. Stay in any one place long enough, and assimilation eventually catches up. You adjust to the world, and even if you don't, the world adjusts to you. To be an immigrant is to be an outsider, which is what Old Colony Mennonites have always wanted. Perhaps migration is less a product of that status than a means of maintaining it. Immigrant identity is etched into their bones. The only things that change are where they're coming from and where they're going.

That night, I go for a beer at 911 Bar on the Plaza de Armas. TVs are tuned to VH1. At eight p.m., four young Mennonites walk in: two men and two women, one boy in jeans and a T-shirt, the other in overalls, the girls both in long-sleeved dresses and white tennis shoes. They sit in the back corner and sip a round of Cuba Libres while watching Michael Jackson cavort across continents in the video for "Black or White." Forty minutes later, they pay up and leave—a weekly tradition, the bartender tells me. He calls them *Menonitas rebeldes*—rebel Mennonites.

Moments later, a rainstorm comes in like a seizure. Water rises biblically in the streets. I finish my beer and drive back out of town, past the *lonchería* and the gas station; past the grocery store with the empty buggy and iron-wheeled John Deere tractor stationed in front like monuments; past the café across the street advertising "Canadian-Style Coffee." The moment I cross the highway, the rain slows to a trickle, then stops completely. The dirt roads are barely even wet. Even the weather knows these are different worlds. Or at least that they're supposed to be.

At the Hotel Fiesta, I fall asleep to the sound of teenagers hooting and whooping and smashing bottles into the gravel, like teenagers do on weekend nights all over Mexico. I can't make out what they're saying, but I know they're speaking German.

# Curry Grows Wherever It Goes

## Ben Mervis

When her sons were young, Ranjit Kaur would often cook them a "scrambled egg" *sabzi*, a Punjabi-inflected dish made with no egg at all, but rather paneer—the fresh, unsalted white cheese common to South Asia. The dish, a household favorite, was so named by her sons because the broken chunks of paneer, turned yellow by spice, bore a striking resemblance to the Western breakfast staple.

Kaur's home cooking was delicate and fresh, often focused around a slew of Asian vegetables rarely found in the local British curry houses of the 1990s, where chicken tikka masala, *balti*, korma, and vindaloo reigned supreme. It was a reflection of the regional tastes and techniques she had learned growing up in the Punjab in northwest India. Here in the UK, she began to make them her own.

Born in 1961 on a farm outside the village of Jandiala, Kaur learned to cook through instruction, osmosis, and expectation. In their modest kitchen, the women of her family taught Kaur the cooking skills that they believed would be valuable to a housewife: how to make the most of cheap staples like lentils; how to judge fruits and vegetables and how to cook the dishes that suited their different states of ripeness. These skills were also important to her faith, Sikhism, which prominently rejects India's traditional caste system and promotes equality through shared communal meals. Kaur married young, at eighteen, and moved with her husband to northern England, where he'd grown up.

A typical lunch spread in Glasgow, Scotland

Four thousand miles apart, the differences between Punjab and
northern England were understandably vast. There was little to relate
cold, inclement Yorkshire to the extreme heat or monsoons of Punjab.
Familiar tastes and favored ingredients like *tinda*, *karela*, and okra were
extremely difficult to find.

Of course, by the time Kaur arrived in Yorkshire, Indian flavors
had been a mainstay of British dining for decades. British interest in

Indian food stretches back hundreds of years, beginning with returning merchants and soldiers of the East India Company and expat members of the social elite. Cookbook writers in the eighteenth and nineteenth centuries, like Elizabeth Acton, Hannah Glasse, and Henrietta Hervey, included Indian recipes in their books; Hervey even dedicated a whole cookbook to Indian cooking. In many cases, though, their recipes for curry read more like fragrant stews: Glasse's recipe for "[chicken] currey the India way" is seasoned with just a spoonful each of turmeric, ginger, and black pepper.

In 1948, British Parliament passed an act allowing all Commonwealth citizens the ability to work in Britain, where a desperate labor shortage had emerged in the wake of World War II. The prospect of economic development and job opportunity brought hundreds of thousands of migrants, chiefly from India and Pakistan, where regional partitions had recently brought political strife and violence, to British shores. The British Sikh community, hailing mostly from the Punjab, grew from an estimated population of seven thousand in 1951 to one hundred forty-four thousand in 1981.

A boom in curry houses followed suit. In fact, the rise of British Indian restaurants dominated the postwar restaurant trade. Between 1960 and 1980, the number of curry houses in England increased tenfold—from three hundred to three thousand. By 1990, that number had doubled. In public opinion polls, chicken tikka masala began to rank above fish and chips as the country's comfort food of choice.

A host of British Indian dishes materialized, often incorporating high levels of spice and generous doses of ghee. Chicken tikka masala was purportedly created by a Glaswegian chef who, attempting to assuage a disgruntled customer, made a curry sauce with a can of Campbell's tomato soup. The heat, grease, and excess of British Indian cooking made it a natural accompaniment for drink-filled evenings and the dinner of choice for leagues of sloshed customers.

Writing for the *Guardian* in 2017, food historian Bee Wilson says, "The curry house taught a white population that was eager to shed its colonial past to relinquish an earlier generation's suspicion of garlic and chili. For a while, curry lovers could tell themselves that openness about spice was a form of cultural broad-mindedness."

Wilson's essay appeared in the wake of the 2016 British referendum to leave the European Union (commonly known as "Brexit"). She lamented that the British fondness for curry did not translate into empathy for the immigrant cooks who formed the backbone of the curry trade. Indeed, curry houses were a talking point for both the "Leave" and "Remain" campaigns, with both sides wondering aloud what would happen if the country didn't address the strict immigration rules for cooks coming from South Asia.

The conversation revolved around cheap labor—prior to the Brexit vote, curry houses were already closing at an alarming rate as the first generation of curry cooks began to retire and struggled to fill their kitchens, because younger generations were seeking out better-paying jobs in engineering and medicine, and immigrant cooks from outside of the EU met insurmountable hurdles to working in the UK. So the debate became a question of whether native-born Brits or EU immigrants could cook a proper curry. But to assume that the great problem posed by Brexit was that it might limit access to cheap labor and "authentic" South Asian flavor is to ignore the far more essential roles that immigrant business owners play in Britain and their local communities. If curry is essential to the British culinary identity—and it is—so, too, are South Asian immigrants to Britain.

In the late eighties, Kaur and her family moved into a house on the ethnically diverse Southside of Glasgow in western Scotland. Historically a working-class city, Glasgow has a proud history of progressive liberalism, and is home to large immigrant communities from Italy, India, Pakistan, Poland, and Romania. However, the city is probably best known for the infamous Glasgow effect: the city's disturbingly high mortality rate from undetermined causes (but generally attributed to poor nutrition).

In Glasgow, Kaur became involved with volunteer work at her local *gurdwara* (Sikh temple). There she performed her *seva* in the temple's community kitchen, or *langar*. The idea of the *seva* is to better the local congregation through voluntary service, often in the form of kitchen duties: cleaning, cooking, or washing dishes. In the *langar*, Kaur worked with other women processing vast quantities of vegetables; her *gurdwara*, like all others, serves free vegetarian meals for all visitors. Everyone is welcome, regardless of race or religion, and everyone dines as equals—together on the floor.

Away from the *gurdwara*, Kaur began to bake large quantities of traditional Punjabi sweets for family occasions: *barfi*—a milk-based confection made with *besan* (gram or chickpea flour)—and *ladoo*—syrupy-sweet balls made with ghee and *besan*, though it can

Kaur taps into the
fundamental human
affection for sweet
things made from dairy.

be made with anything from coconut to rice, lentil, or nut flours.
Kaur's confections gained a following among friends and extended
family, and in time she began receiving large orders for her sweets
and samosas.

Prep work became a family affair. Gurjit, Kaur's middle son,
would return home from university to join a queue of helpers peeling potatoes around the kitchen table. Soon conversations turned to
the prospect of something more permanent. Gurjit and his brothers
encouraged their mother to find a brick-and-mortar space of her own,
a restaurant that she could use as an extension of her kitchen table.

Despite the ubiquity of curry houses, Glasgow lacked a vegetarian Indian restaurant.

Ranjit's Kitchen opened in 2015, and quickly succeeded in attracting a broad range of customers. It's equally common to dine beside elderly Indian men, young Western families, and hipster students. The restaurant's interior doesn't feel overtly or cliché Indian. (There are no pictures of the Taj Mahal here.) But there is a warmth to the interior: long wooden trestle tables are lined up in rows for communal dining, and the walls are brightly painted with a pattern inspired by traditional *phulkari* ("flower work") embroidery typical of Punjab. Gurjit serves as the restaurant manager. His brothers, Jag and Hardeep, and cousin Talisha help him run the restaurant. Ranjit is in charge of the kitchen, aided by four family friends: Sarbjit, Sarbjit, Hari, and Liam.

At Ranjit's there are no airs or graces, no tablecloths, fancy cutlery, or formal service. The food arrives all at once. In some ways it recalls a *dhaba*, one of the countless roadside cafés in India that cater to working-class stiffs with plates of simple Punjabi curries and rounds of fresh roti. Flatbreads are the primary accompaniment to the restaurant's main dishes. Roti are made from whole-grain wheat and fired in round *tava* pans that are also used for frying *paratha*—pliable flatbread stuffed with potato, radish, or cauliflower, or served sweet with an addictive sugary glaze.

Ranjit's menu is short, featuring a rotating selection of daal (spiced lentils) and *sabzi* (stewed vegetables). Kaur's *sabzi* begin with a base of onions, cumin, garlic, ginger, green chilies, and sometimes fenugreek, to which she adds vegetables like cauliflower and potato (for *aloo gobi*) or spinach (for *saag*). The curries are homely, and fiery chili is notably absent. They are fragrant and delicately spiced, slow-cooked in thin gravies, and heavy on the vegetables.

The restaurant makes its own homemade paneer on a daily basis, and serves it tossed with garden peas, broken into chunks in a sweet and spicy mixture of chickpeas and peppers, or in the family-favorite "scrambled" paneer. Ranjit's *paneer pakora* features slices of the white cheese sandwiched around tomato relish, dipped in a fluffy gram flour batter, and lightly fried.

Kaur's famous samosas are also present on the menu, as are her *barfi*. The latter come in small squares with cups of coffee, taking the place of the traditional Scottish tablet, a dense and intensely sugary treat that accompanies tea and coffee in cafés throughout the

Scrambled egg *sabzi* taps into nostalgia from one part of the world with ingredients from another.

country. The *barfi*, in comparison, have a tempered sweetness and a texture like soft, crumbly fudge.

"Some customers are coming in and having a *thali* [plate] with a different daal or *sabzi* every day, and to me that's beautiful, because they're eating the way that we eat," says Gurjit, who pulls double-duty as his mother's preferred spokesperson. "When we grew up, we always had daal, *sabzi*, and rotis, and sometimes as kids you moaned about it—you wanted to eat potato waffles or frozen crap—but now I'm seeing other people asking for the daal or the *sabzi*, and they're happy to eat it two or three or four times a week."

In a city characterized by a general distrust of vegetables, Ranjit's Kitchen has managed to endear its customers to varieties of plants both familiar and foreign. Gurjit recalls his mother telling him as a kid, "People here don't know how to cook, that's why they eat rubbish. People don't see how you can turn cauliflower and potato, two things that are readily available in this country, into an interesting dish."

Customers often draw the connection between vegetables at the restaurant and what they've seen in the neighborhood's South Asian grocers. "They tell us, 'I've seen them in the shops,'" says Gurjit. "But they've never known what to do with them." Return customers are sometimes invited to try off-menu curries made with more challenging ingredients like bitter gourds and sweet rice.

The restaurant's success has moved Kaur to donate money to local charities. Once Ranjit's recovers their initial setup costs, they've decided to make charity work a core part of their business by donating a larger portion of their profits to local and national charities, as well as groups back in the Punjab.

Curry's story is a globalized one. It pulls together gastronomic features plucked from disparate cultures—chilies from the Americas, spices from all over South Asia, vinegar from Portuguese colonists. There are hundreds of regional variations in India, Pakistan, and Bangladesh, not to mention distinctive versions in countries like Japan, Thailand, South Africa, Jamaica, Macau (by way of Portugal), and, of course, the United Kingdom. As of 2016, there were more than twelve thousand curry houses in the UK—the question of curry's place in British cuisine is long settled.

Curry is a product and reflection of cultural openness. It continues to evolve wherever it goes, enriching the cuisine of each new home, including the colorful crossroads city of postindustrial Glasgow.

"I love that we've created a space that demonstrates everything that's good about immigration," says Gurjit. "A space that demonstrates everything good about sharing your culture, about coming together and sharing what you have as a family and as a community. That's something we should all be proud of."

# Your Fire and My Fire Burn the Same

Arielle Johnson

Since the emergence of our earliest human ancestors—the flint knife–wielding *Homo habilis*—2.6 million years ago, our evolution has been driven by food and the technology we've developed to prepare it.

Bone and fossil data show that when *Homo erectus* evolved from *Homo habilis* about 1.9 million years ago, changes to our ancestors' diet corresponded with major changes in anatomy that persist to the present day. As the *Homo* brain became larger and teeth became smaller, it became impossible for the species to subsist on a diet of raw food. Some kind of processing was required to make food more easily digestible.

One of those processing techniques may have been fermentation, a favored method in the traditional cuisines of the Arctic regions, as well as in the early preparation of tubers like cassava. Fermentation is easily achievable with resources that were accessible to *Homo erectus*, such as a hole in the ground, or a pond and some rocks.

Another foundational technique of human development is cooking with fire. Despite what your local raw foodist might say, the human species cannot survive on fresh, uncooked food: vegetarian, omnivorous, or otherwise. Our species is obliged to live on cooked food, and cooking happens everywhere, every day, at every level of cuisine. Setting wood on fire and harnessing its heat to transform the raw into the roasted, boiled, caramelized, grilled,

Much like everywhere else on earth, people in Mongolia use fire to warm food, water, and themselves.

seared, softened, steamed, or otherwise cooked is common to every culture on earth.

Fire is undeniably an essential culinary technology, but it's unclear for exactly how long it's been around. Evolutionary biologist Richard Wrangham lays out some very persuasive arguments that cooking was employed as early as two million years ago by *Homo erectus*. Meanwhile, some archaeologists are loath to accept a date earlier than one hundred twenty-five thousand years ago as the official beginning of widespread fire mastery, around the same time that our species, *Homo sapiens*, emerged. So far, the earliest indisputable evidence of fire use—which we can't yet distinguish as "handy fire making" or "opportunistic wildfire capture"—dates to one million years ago, in the Wonderwerk Cave in South Africa. After that, groups of *Homo erectus*, *Homo neanderthalensis*, and other ancient cousins to *Homo sapiens* were using fire frequently in present-day Africa, Europe, and Asia.

Cooking over a wood fire engages us with some of the most deeply embedded parts of our humanness. It feels beautifully straightforward—just wood, food, and heat—but it would be a mistake to think of it as simple or elemental. In fact, burning a piece of wood involves about a half dozen totally separate chemical processes, each with at least several, if not hundreds or thousands of, discrete component reactions. There's combustion itself, which includes the formation of flame, blackbody radiation, and spectral line emission; there's the smoldering and pyrolysis of the wood, two separate processes that get the wood ready to become fuel for combustion; and there's the formation of smoke, a hugely complex mixture of volatile molecules, molecules in solution, and particulate matter.

All this is to say that building a fire is one of the most chemically complex processes one can enact. It is an elaborate choreography that cooks everywhere understand intuitively, but few grasp on an intellectual level.

So let's have a look, beginning with the basics.

Strictly speaking, fire (or combustion) is a process, not a thing: at its heart, it's a very fast chemical oxidation reaction between oxygen and a fuel, such as hydrogen or methane, resulting in heat and waste products, such as carbon dioxide. In any chemical reaction, you start with certain molecules and end up with different ones. The molecules you start with are called reactants—as in, they react with one another. The molecules you end up with are the products. In a combustion reaction, oxygen grabs electrons from other reactant molecules, creating product molecules with a different electron distribution. This electron grabbing is highly exothermic, meaning it releases energy in the form of light and heat.

A flame is the visible part of fire, a result of the reactant (oxygen, hydrogen, methane, etc.) and product (carbon dioxide, etc.) gases being superheated by the energy released during combustion. The various shades of flame are produced when electrons in the fuel absorb energy, get excited, and temporarily jump into a higher-energy quantum state. When they fall back down to their usual quantum state, they release the energy required to make the jump in the form of light—the wavelength (color) of which is determined by how far they fall (the energy gap). Different atoms and molecules have distinct energy gaps, and give off distinct wavelengths of light, their emission spectra.

If the fire is a shade of blue, you're dealing with a totally gaseous fuel, like hydrogen, methane, or propane, that is well supplied with oxygen—a purer fire, if you will. An orange flame is derived from a more complex fuel source (wood, for instance) or a fire that is low in oxygen; these fires produce a lot of impurities and waste products like soot, which don't get totally burned but rather form minute particles that get carried up into the flame and emit colored light through a process called blackbody radiation.

A Patagonian
asado

Flames get their teardrop shape from convection and gravity: hotter gases travel upward, and fresh, cooler oxygen gets drawn into the bottom of the flame. Without gravity (in space, for instance), flames are spherical.

Flames only occur when a gaseous fuel is combusting. But wood is obviously not a gas, so how does it burn?

It comes down to a process called pyrolysis. At the base of a fire, where there is the least oxygen and temperatures are lower, you can see the wood turning black. That's pyrolysis, a form of high-heat decomposition. As wood is heated, the water in it evaporates and the wood goes from being *potentially* burnable to *actually* burnable, changing from a bunch of lignin, cellulose, hemicellulose, water, resin, and sap into fairly pure carbon (charcoal), flammable tars (phenols, guaiacols, furans, and other products), and vapors (methane, propane, other hydrocarbons, carbon monoxide, methanol, acetone, and acetic acid).

Moving in from the blackened wood, you reach the glowing embers of the fire, where the newly formed charcoal is smoldering. Smoldering is a slower form of combustion in which oxygen is reacting directly with the solid surface. The speed and heat of the smoldering reaction are much lower compared to the speed and heat of fire (aka flaming combustion) because the amount of oxygen and fuel that can be combined is limited by the surface area of the charcoal.

Finally, you have the flame, where the flammable gases and vapors produced by pyrolysis are reacting rapidly with oxygen to produce heat and light. The smoke rising above the fire is another product of pyrolysis—a complex mixture of vapors, dissolved tars (guaiacol gives smoke its smoky smell), tiny solid particles of pure carbon, polycyclic aromatic hydrocarbons, and ash. As more of the wood is transformed by pyrolysis into charcoal and flammable gases, the fire burns cleaner, with less smoke. This may already be apparent to grill cooks who spend their nights in front of a flaming hearth, but the hottest part of the fire is the flame, followed by the smoldering embers, followed by the blackening charcoal.

But temperature alone isn't the whole story. When you're talking about cooking, both heat and temperature come into play, and they are, in fact, different things. Both are measures of energy, but where heat is an overall measure of energy, the more familiar concept of temperature is better described as heat concentration or heat density. Consider, by way of analogy, a shot glass of whiskey and a glass of wine.

Both contain the same amount of pure alcohol, but the whiskey is more concentrated. Heat is like the amount of pure alcohol you have, and temperature is like the concentration of alcohol in your glass. Heat and temperature are coupled, but they're separate dials both at your disposal to fine-tune your cooking.

Let me explain. Cooking is basically the transfer of energy in the form of heat from one thing to another. The total amount of energy transferred from the fuel to the food determines how cooked the food becomes. How fast it cooks and what kinds of chemical reactions occur on the surface of the food is where temperature plays a bigger role. Food exposed to a very high temperature will cook, then caramelize, then Maillardize, then begin to pyrolize into charcoal before the heat has made much headway into the raw interior. Lower temperatures will slow the rate of heat transfer and create an entirely different effect.

Cooking is a constant tinkering of two knobs: (1) the total amount of heat you want transferred to your food, and (2) the temperature at which you transfer that heat. When it comes to cooking over fire, these can be controlled by choosing the type of fuel, the type of combustion, and the route through which the heat is transferred from the fuel to the food.

Will you set up your fire for flaming or smoldering combustion? Will you expose your ingredients directly to the flames or coals, or will you channel the flow of energy through an intermediary like a metal pan or clay pot and use conductive heat transfer? The pan or pot will never reach the same temperature as the flame, but it will absorb the flame's heat and spread it out over a larger area, delivering a bunch of heat at a lower temperature than a direct flame or ember.

Do you want to encourage pyrolized smoky flavors? You could do this by allowing the smoke to deposit on the food. If you're cooking over charcoal, you could add a little wood, like a smoky condiment. Juices from food that fall onto coals also pyrolize and quickly break up into smaller flavor molecules, delivering a lighter perfume of self-made smoke. If you're cooking over a gas fire, this juice-smoke is the sole source of smoky flavors—of course, since meat juices and wood are quite different chemically and structurally, they produce very different flavors of smoke.

From the same basic process of wood fire, there are countless directions cooks can go. You could load a Weber or ceramic *kamado*-style grill with charcoal, or fire up an offset smoker, or set up an *asado*-style grill with a firebox or *brasero*. It's a wonder to behold all the ways humans have refined and manipulated fire, but it's really even more incredible to think that no matter what the setup, we're all performing the same process our ancestors used millions of years ago: converting carbon and oxygen into heat.

Pitmaster Rodney Scott infuses pork with the flavor of pyrolized wood.

# Fried Chicken Is Common Ground

## Osayi Endolyn

Before he started cooking hot chicken in Australia, before he opened his fifth location of Belles Hot Chicken and began planning for expansion in Asia, before he was serving customers like Chance the Rapper and American football star Marshawn Lynch, Morgan McGlone was sitting on a porch in Nashville.

McGlone and friends were eating hot chicken, cooling their lips with glasses of natural wine, when he thought, *This is how I should make my living.* After an itinerant decade of cooking around the world and three years learning from American chef Sean Brock, McGlone was struck with the idea of bringing Nashville's most famous dish together with his love for wild-fermented wines and selling it to the audience he knew best: Australians.

But, of course, long before McGlone thought to make money from American-style fried chicken, there were many, many others.

For at least a hundred and fifty years, people have been cooking and selling fried chicken in America. The earliest were black women, newly freed from slavery after the Emancipation Proclamation of 1863. These entrepreneurial cooks, known as "waiter carriers," brought their skills and their chicken to markets and train stations to sell to travelers passing through towns like Gordonsville, Virginia. They sold chicken to support themselves and their families, because that was the work that was available to them.

Though their culinary contributions went uncredited for centuries, African and African American cooks were largely responsible for creating what Americans now know as Southern food. From the mid-eighteenth century through Emancipation, dishes like fried chicken were developed and prepared by enslaved cooks, who combined West African culinary traditions with those of indigenous North American peoples and European colonialists.

In the early nineteenth century, white members of high society like Mary Randolph, a distant relative to Thomas Jefferson, wrote cookbooks that commandeered the recipes of black cooks. The books were a revelation to white audiences at the time and helped launch dishes like fried chicken into widespread popularity. Meanwhile, notes writer Adrian Miller in his book *Soul Food: The Surprising Story of an American Cuisine One Plate at a Time*, African Americans who perfected this dish under inhumane conditions were subject to repugnant stereotypes about their affinity for fried chicken. After being forced through servitude to cook for landowners, and later relegated by circumstance to sell fried chicken for a living, African Americans were depicted in advertisements, postcards, newspapers, and flyers as chicken thieves and animalistic consumers of fried chicken—images and stereotypes that persist today. It's why many black people in America still refuse to eat fried chicken in public, carrying the stigma with them even if they've never seen the images in person.

In spite of these indignities, fried chicken didn't disappear within black communities. In fact, it spread even farther as part of the six-decades-long Great Migration, during which at least six million African Americans fled a turbulent and segregated South to start anew in northern and western cities. As scholar Psyche Williams-Forson documented in *Building Houses Out of Chicken Legs: Black Women, Food, and Power*, these men, women, and children were prohibited from using most train accommodations along their trip, so they prepared fried chicken from recipes designed to withstand the long journey, boxed it up cold, and carried it on board for sustenance. When they arrived in their new homes, fried chicken was a special Sunday meal—a place it occupied for much of the early twentieth century.

Then, a few years after World War II, Harland Sanders turned a single restaurant in Kentucky, where he served pressure-fried chicken, into a full-fledged franchise business under the name Kentucky Fried Chicken. By marketing his restaurants using his symbolic status as a nonmilitary "Colonel," along with a heavy dose of imagery that evoked

Hot chicken has grown into a global phenomenon, but it began life in Nashville, Tennessee, at restaurants like Bolton's Spicy Chicken & Fish.

slavery-era plantations, he grew Kentucky Fried Chicken into a multi-million-dollar company. Later, after Sanders had mostly stepped away from the business, KFC would swell into the world's second largest restaurant brand, with locations in more than one hundred countries. KFC's success (along with that of Church's and Popeyes) brought a version of Southern fried chicken to a global audience.

Almost seventy years after the Colonel opened his first franchise, and a century and a half after Emancipation, McGlone, an affable half-Maori, half-Irish sous-chef working for one of America's most celebrated Southern chefs, decided that fried chicken and natural wine was a pairing that needed to happen. He flew to Australia armed with a recipe and a business plan.

All of this, for better or worse, is possible because fried chicken is unequivocally, fundamentally delicious. At various periods throughout history, fried chicken has been craved, rejected, heralded, excoriated, belittled, honored, and exploited—often all at once. The dish's exact origins are hard to pin down and, perhaps, beside the point. A quick survey of the food world reveals that practically every culture that eats chicken has come up with a way to crisp birds in hot oil.

In addition to the bone-in, breaded, and skillet-fried chicken ubiquitous in the United States, there's twice-fried Korean fried chicken with gochujang; adobo-rubbed chicken in the Guatemalan tradition; Japanese *karaage* seasoned with soy, ginger, and garlic; Brazilian fried chicken, Chinese fried chicken, Thai fried chicken, and a Keralan American mash-up with cilantro, mint, and serrano peppers popularized in Atlanta, Georgia, by chef and cookbook author Asha Gomez. At grocery stores, gas stations, walk-up windows, and fine dining restaurants, fried chicken is served in buckets and baskets, as sandwiches, wraps, biscuits, nuggets, tenders, fingers, and wings. A US trade association estimated that Americans would consume 1.35 billion chicken wings in a single day: the 2018 Super Bowl. Many of them were no doubt served Buffalo-style: deep-fried and tossed in hot sauce, with a creamy blue cheese dressing and batons of celery and carrot on the side.

In 1945, in a black neighborhood of Nashville called Hadley Park, Thornton Prince opened Prince's BBQ Chicken Shack—today, known as Prince's Hot Chicken—the first-ever hot chicken establishment. The name "hot chicken" is a charmingly matter-of-fact and apropos descriptor of the dish: chicken breast, legs, or wings dredged in flour and fried, then bombarded with a proprietary blend of dry seasonings (secret spice rubs abound when it comes to fried chicken) that always includes a heavy dose of cayenne pepper. It's customarily served atop slices of squishy-soft white bread to absorb the chicken fat and scarlet-red seasoning, with sweet cucumber pickles on the side.

An evening and late-night haunt, Prince's built its reputation by serving the city's African American population, but white customers began to pay attention after the restaurant moved to a downtown location. In the decades since, Prince's, along with numerous copycats, have become tourist destinations in the city and throughout the United States. Nashville now has a Hot Chicken Festival. And in 2016, KFC started serving its rendition of hot chicken in more than four thousand US locations.

McGlone tasted his first hot chicken in 2012 at a Prince's-inspired restaurant in Nashville called 400 Degrees. He'd recently been promoted to chef de cuisine of Husk Nashville, the sibling to Chef Brock's celebrated New Southern restaurant in Charleston, South Carolina. Before arriving in the American South, McGlone had spent the preceding decade in and out of the culinary world, cooking for chefs like Alex Atala in São Paulo and Pierre Gagnaire in Paris. But he also put in time working on the sets of photo shoots, and as a security escort and talent scout in the upper echelons of the fashion world, amassing more than his fair share of hilarious, terrifying, and outrageous experiences involving Russian models, P Diddy's New Year's Eve party, rock stars, and an original Picasso.

Like many chefs, McGlone is a wanderer. New Zealand is his birth country, but he has rarely stayed in one place for long. He credits Brock's impassioned advocacy of Southern food for luring him to the region and keeping him there for three and a half years.

"I used to think that Southern cuisine was just fried chicken and barbecue, but it's actually an incredibly refined way of cooking that's taken its influences from the Huguenots, from the Jewish settlers, and especially in Charleston, from the Gullah people," explains McGlone.

Southern cuisine is, in fact, a cuisine that is *especially* black—African—in that the food was grown, cultivated, processed, improved, prepared, and served by West African people and their descendants. "It's not from my culture," he says. "I just gravitated toward it."

In many places, but particularly in America, this is where things can get tricky. Anyone can gravitate toward a culture, and "Southern culture" contains a sprawling, nebulous multitude: everyone from trap rappers to rural squirrel hunters will talk about their love for the culture, land, and food of the South. But it's easy to misappropriate culture, too. There is a distinct pattern in the United States, wherein African American chefs struggle to find parity with their white counterparts in terms of recognition, funding, and reward. Both codified and unspoken social policies ensured that the black women who worked as waiter carriers in the nineteenth century never saw their business become a global franchise.

Brock, McGlone's mentor, has had to walk a careful line in trying to show appreciation and deference to the black Southern cooks who came before him while still becoming a prominent proponent. And while Brock grew up in the South, McGlone is one step further removed—an immigrant of Polynesian and European descent, who sells hot chicken on the other side of the world.

McGlone is a talented chef. He's beloved all across the restaurant world. He has studied the nuanced levels of hot chicken spiciness, the benefits of flour hydration, and how oil temperature affects the crispness of his chicken. He acknowledges the lineage of black American entrepreneurs who invented and popularized hot chicken. He is an engaged citizen of the world, who speaks four languages. His chicken has won dedicated fans from Australia as well as visitors from America and other parts of the globe. He is proud to say his beans, greens, and macaroni and cheese are faithful to the recipes he learned in the South. He likes to feed people, and to eat his cooking is a joyful thing.

But American fried chicken will always be tied inextricably to race and the violent, egregious exploitation of black Americans. Outside of the United States, this complex food can seem dissociated from its history.

"First they want to make sure that it's delicious," says McGlone of his diners at Belles. "And then they want to make sure that it has provenance, and then they want to make sure that it's a continuation, that it means something."

And there, McGlone has landed on the two questions that give all food consequence: Is it tasty? And does it mean something?

With fried chicken, the taste question is moot. Vegetarians notwithstanding, everyone loves fried chicken. Some fried chicken is better than others, but even bad fried chicken is better than none. Everyone who wants to cook fried chicken should. Everyone who wants to sell American-style fried chicken ought to be able to give the market a try. Fried chicken is eaten all over the planet. People from completely opposite sides of the socioeconomic and political spectrum, who might agree on almost nothing, can agree that fried chicken is good.

And so, with its deliciousness unquestionable, all that remains is what fried chicken means. No matter where it's cooked, American fried chicken carries the learning and effort and skill of a people who persevered against unfathomable odds. That Southern hue follows fried chicken all the way to Melbourne and Sydney, too. And therein lies an incredible opportunity. If everyone can agree to share fried chicken, then perhaps that's a step toward sharing the weight of its complex legacy as well.

# One Seed Rules Them All

Tienlon Ho

The sesame seed is a foundation of civilization, one of humanity's oldest cultivated crops, but when I was growing up in the Corn Belt of the United States, it was primarily known as "those white things on burger buns."

In those pale, teardrop-shaped flecks, it was hard to detect the nutty flavor that I found in the toasted oil my mother drizzled into the dough for her *cong you bing*, scallion pancakes. They tasted only vaguely like the black seeds from the Persian market, which we toasted and ground, then sipped as *zhi ma hu*, sesame porridge, or rolled into the sweet centers of *tang yuan*, soft rice-flour dumplings. We used *zhi ma jiang*, an umber paste of ground sesame, to flavor sauces for everything from noodles to hot pot. Only later, once I began eating falafel slathered in garlicky tahini sauce on late nights in college, did I draw the connection from tahini to *zhi ma* to the idle garnish on the burgers of my youth.

Sesame is everywhere. It has come to represent a great deal to a great many different cooks around the world. But in spite of all its many variations in appearance, flavor, and application, the sesame in all the world's oils, pastes, and bread toppings is one and the same species: *Sesamum indicum*, first cultivated in the Indus Valley at Harappa (current-day Pakistan) some four thousand years ago.

Wild sesame began as a small, black seed, likely in Africa, but it changed in size and color as it moved around the world. It prefers tropical heat and sun but can adapt to grow in cooler climes, even in thin soil, so long as there is occasional rain. Through human intervention, sesame was bred into either spindly plants with small, waxy leaves or squat plants with full leaves, each producing seeds that appeal to varied tastes.

The flavor of cultivated sesame seeds ranges from somewhat milky and floral for lighter varieties to earthier, more complex, and smokier in darker ones. The seed coat, or hull, is what makes sesame black, white, or shades of brown, red, and gold. White varieties fetch the highest price on today's market because they are thought to be the oiliest and have the most complex flavor. But in Sudan, red seeds are thought to be the richest, and in Japan, black are preferred for their deep flavor. So far, scientists have cataloged and stored more than twenty-five thousand varieties of sesame from India and China—each with its own drought tolerance, pest resistance, nutritional content, color, size, and flavor. In ancient India, sesame was a talisman, a food of longevity. It was scattered beneath the beds of the sick and offered to Hindu gods and deceased ancestors. Sesame is about half fat and one-fifth protein, and loaded with calcium, iron, and other vital minerals. It is so nourishing that Buddha himself was said to have survived on rice porridge skimmings topped with a dash of sesame oil each day. As he approached enlightenment, his daily diet narrowed to a single precious sesame seed.

Humans have historically consumed sesame mostly in the form of oil. When pressed from untoasted seeds, the pale gold oil has a high smoke point and neutral flavor. Toasted sesame produces oil that is dark amber and robust, and is used most commonly as a dressing rather than a cooking agent. An insult still used in parts of India today is *jartila*, or "wild sesame," so coined because wild seeds give little oil. A *jartila* is a good-for-nothing.

Thousands of years ago, sesame traveled west from India to Mesopotamia, Egypt, Greece, and Rome, and east to China and the rest of Asia, because it is both nourishing and portable. It does not turn rancid crossing great deserts. Its only downside comes at harvest. Once ripe, sesame pods snap open with a pop, scattering the treasure within (a feature said to be the inspiration for Ali Baba's magic incantation, "Open, sesame!"). To capture the tiny seeds, the stalks must be pulled while the pods are still green, dried in bundles, then shaken or hit with sticks before the chaff is winnowed away. Nearly all sesame comes from India, Sudan, China, Myanmar, and Nigeria, where it is still harvested as it has been since the beginning—by hand, by the poor and often subjugated.

Sesame crossed the Atlantic to the Americas in the early seventeenth century with enslaved West Africans, who knew the seed as benne. They soaked the seeds to release their oil, then ground them into mash for stews and paste for bread. Benne flourished in slaves' gardens from the Carolinas down to Jamaica, but it would be another three centuries before it took widespread hold in North America. The breeding of a sesame variety that could be harvested mechanically by combine and a patent for hulling seeds with chemical solvents finally gave sesame mass commercial appeal. McDonald's Big Mac and its spongy, sesame-speckled bun arrived in the United States in 1967.

Like people, with enough time, food that was once foreign can eventually become so entrenched in a culture that it endows that culture with a new heritage. A dish can feel of one place, while being from another. Sesame-seed buns, for instance, have deep roots outside of the United States. In the Levant, on the western edge of ancient Mesopotamia, people ate sesame-adorned breads long before the region was carved into nations. One form, known as *ka'ak*, is typically leavened with fermented chickpeas, shaped into rings, and baked. They are made savory in Israel but glazed with milk and sugar in Lebanon. Iraqis favor a version with raisins. In Greece and Turkey, it is made flatter and known as *koulouri* or *simit*, the latter of which is sometimes sweetened with grape molasses. Arab vendors arrived in China's cities around 600 CE, hawking sesame-topped breads like these and *manakish*, another flatbread topped with za'atar, a spice blend containing sesame seeds. The Hui minority carry on the tradition in China with *shao bing*—rounds of flaky, layered bread heavily adorned with sesame and often stuffed with savory fillings. Like its makers, these breads are all related, and yet each has its particularities.

There are likewise countless plays on sesame as a seasoning. Throughout the Middle East, white sesame seeds are blended with sumac, thyme, marjoram, salt, and other spices particular to whoever is making the za'atar. In Japan, sesame features in *gomashio* (sesame and salt), *furikake* (dried fish and seaweed), and *shichimi togarashi* (black

Humans have a remarkable ability to agree on hummus's deliciousness while disagreeing about everything else.

and white sesame with chili, numbing *sansho* pepper, orange peel, ginger, and seaweed). Sierra Leone's version of sesame seasoning is *ogiri-saro*, which is made by fermenting seeds left over from making oil. The resulting paste is smoked, wrapped in Christmas bush or banana leaves, then smoked again until soft and pungent, and used to enliven stews. Indonesia's *cabuk* is a sauce of seeds cured in rice-straw ash and blended with salt, garlic, and chili.

Sesame confections also span the globe. Halva, an airy blend of kneaded sesame and syrup, has many forms, but is often mixed with the local flavors of the region—from pistachios in Istanbul to orange in Thessaloniki. Halva traveled from the Balkans and the Middle East with Jewish immigrants, who made it popular in Poland and Romania in the nineteenth century and trendy in Brooklyn today. As Syrian immigrants found their way to places as far-flung as Rio de Janeiro, specialties like halva with Brazil nuts appeared.

Sesame paste is known as tahini in Israel, *rashi* in Iraq, *ardeh* in Iran, *tahin* in Turkey, and *tashi* on Cyprus, and it is all made more or less the same way: the kernels of sesame seeds are separated from their hulls, then roasted and ground. A smooth and creamy texture is favored in the Middle East, while a thicker grain is preferred around the Mediterranean. Tahini can be simply seasoned with lemon juice and eaten with bread, or spread on meat and fish. It is used to balance out fatty proteins or add heft to potatoes or greens. Lamb *siniyah*, a Palestinian dish, involves using tahini as a crust for roasting, creating a flavorful, edible exterior around superbly succulent meat.

On good days, our shared taste for sesame can erase political boundaries. Some of the best tahini in the world is made in the outskirts of Nablus, the second-largest city in the West Bank, where the oldest Palestinian-run tahini factories import sesame seeds from Ethiopia and mill them between basalt grinding stones from Syria. Tahini is so vital to Israelis that rabbis monitor the factories by remote camera to certify the production methods as kosher, since they cannot enter parts of the city by law. Some West Bank producers even enjoy special entry permits and open access to Ben Gurion Airport. To make tahini, after all, water and oil must be mixed until they come together to form a cohesive blend.

On the other hand, sesame can be a lightning rod for lawsuits and flame wars over who has the right to claim ownership over certain foods. Cooks in nearly every country in the Middle East, from Jordan to Syria, Iraq, Lebanon, Egypt, Palestine, and Israel, steadfastly assert ownership over hummus. Israelis and Lebanese in particular have grappled over the dish, which is, in its simplest form, chickpeas blended with tahini. The fighting has ranged from arguments over food labels describing hummus as a "traditional Israeli snack" to a duel over the Guinness World Record for the largest hummus plate. There have been consumer boycotts, a copyright infringement suit, and an EU petition.

In 2014, the dip company Sabra, which is co-owned by the Israeli Strauss conglomerate and PepsiCo, petitioned the US Food and Drug Administration to define hummus as a spread made with chickpeas and at least 5 percent tahini. In its petition, Sabra cited recipes published in Cairo in the thirteenth century, the etymology of the word *hummus* (it is short for *hummus bi tahini*, or "chickpeas with sesame paste" in Arabic), and cited Fat-Free Roasted Red Pepper hummus as a travesty in Exhibit B. It was a move to edge out the competition for the growing hummus market in the United States ($1 billion in annual sales and counting), but it was also an attempt to define the right way—and the right people—to make hummus. The FDA has yet to rule on the petition.

But sesame has existed for longer than modern political divides and ancient kingdoms. It serves as a symbol of cultural identity because it is such a vital ingredient to so many cuisines, but the truth is that it grew into its distinctive forms because of the diversity of the people who have nurtured it, and it has endured in recipes because of the strength of the people who cook with it.

Like people, sesame will adapt wherever it takes root. It will grow and change until it becomes a part of its new home. Some varieties grow faster so they can survive dry climates, while others ripen slowly so they can withstand storms. Some seeds grow bitter and more nourishing, and others turn light and sweet. They may look different, but when you peel the skin away, underneath, they're all the same seed.

# If It Does Well Here, It Belongs Here

René Redzepi

When we opened our restaurant, Noma, fifteen years ago, we told ourselves that our goal was to explore the Nordic region. That was the whole premise behind our cooking—there wasn't more to it than that.

At first, we thought it was all about ingredients—finding the right ones, cutting out the rest. My partner in the kitchen at the time, Mads Refslund, and I had these elaborate ideas about how we'd preserve things in season and never use imported herbs or spices. We wanted to keep everything completely pure, insisting that all our food be grown nearby. We decided that vegetables like tomatoes, which have a Mediterranean identity and require a hot climate, wouldn't fit into our style of cooking. It wasn't because we disliked tomatoes. One of my best childhood memories is of picking a tomato in the courtyard of our home in Macedonia, sinking my teeth into it, and, for the next twenty minutes, slowly drinking the liquid from the inside until nothing was left but a man-made tomato raisin.

Everything we did in those early days was built around a blind search for identity—not necessarily a deliberate one, but one driven by a longing to anchor ourselves to something. We'd eventually alter these constraints, but committing ourselves to extreme locality ended up being an incredible process for us to go through. Our appreciation for wild food and foraging emerged from this restriction. As we

A cook from Denmark gathers ingredients in Australia.

became familiar with the ingredients around us and the way minute changes in the weather dictated their quality, the next logical step was to go into nature to find things for ourselves.

There was something about foraging that I really connected with. At my previous job, the chef collected wild ramps and mushrooms, but on a very small scale—nothing more than the foraging the average Scandinavian does. The act of going outside and finding food in its natural setting seemed to tap into something else in me.

I grew up hearing all these French or Italian or Spanish chefs talking about their grandmother's cooking and the beautiful moment in her kitchen when they knew they would become a cook. I always thought these stories were overly romanticized, maybe even untrue. Could it really be that everybody had an incredible cook for a grandmother? Were none of the great chefs forced into this profession because the cooking they grew up with was such shit?

I began thinking back to my own childhood. We were a poor Albanian farming family living in Macedonia, and when all the grownups were working in the fields, the kids were roaming about, picking berries and wild chestnuts. I grew up foraging. There wasn't a word for it—we just thought of it as playing. But as an adult, I began to see the charms of my own upbringing, and realized that the higher value we tend to place on certain cultural narratives doesn't mean that lesser-known stories are any less vital.

We're still in the midst of the journey we began when Noma first opened. We're still figuring out what it means to be a cook in this part of the world. Our original idea to use only local products eventually started to collapse under the weight of new questions: When is an ingredient truly local? What makes it belong here? What does it take for an ingredient to be integrated to the point where you think, *Now I can put it on the menu. Now it makes sense?*

If you go far enough back in time, you'll find that almost everything in your everyday pantry actually came from somewhere else. Over time, we began to understand that an ingredient like cardamom has a thousand-year-old history in the region. Why deprive ourselves of it? Why take cinnamon away? Ground ginger, an ingredient born in South Asia, is a huge part of traditional Danish baking. Most Scandinavians are intimately familiar with the flavor—we consider it ours.

It's not just ingredients, either—ideas can take root and grow as well. I've spent a lot of time in Mexico over the past ten years, and I've learned to think of chili heat like a flavor. It's not only this sensation

that burns your mouth. Once you've opened your mind to the different nuances of various chilies, you realize that harnessing spiciness is the same as working with umami or playing with acidity. And once you learn how to use it, it becomes a sixth basic taste, on par with saltiness, sweetness, and bitterness. Spiciness doesn't play a big role in Nordic cuisine, but why would I not allow myself to use a sixth flavor when I know it's out there? It doesn't matter that it wasn't here fifty years ago, or even five years ago. It could lead to something great.

The same questions can be asked about people. Until the age of ten, I considered Macedonia my home country. The Yugoslav Wars brought an end to that, and then Denmark became home,

although much of my childhood was spent journeying back and forth between the two. As a young cook, travel was an essential part of the experience—to cook in the best kitchens, you have to leave home. And recently, if I take into account the time we've spent doing pop-ups in Japan, Mexico, and Australia over the past three years, I've probably only lived in Denmark half the time. It makes me wonder, *Am I Scandinavian? Am I local to this place?*

The way I see things today, if something grows here, it belongs here. If a Mexican farmer gives us a seed and we put it in the ground in Denmark and something delicious emerges, I say, welcome to the family.

We're fortunate at Noma to have a lot of people who want to work with us. Our cooks and *stagiaires* come from all over the world. Many people find it very difficult to figure out how to fit in when they first arrive, but if you can learn how to navigate an environment with people from dozens of countries—if you can understand and sift through all those different opinions and demeanors—you'll do fine anywhere you go.

That being said, it's not just our cooks' responsibility to find their own way. If we want our people to succeed, we have to make them feel comfortable. It's very important to allow them—especially those cooks who come from elsewhere—to have some time to find their footing. They will do whatever the job takes, but we must set the tone for them.

I used to deal personally with acclimating all the incoming cooks. We would sit down and talk about whatever was bothering them, whether they'd found a place to live, how their colleagues were treating them. But some people would never open up to me because I'm their chef. I couldn't get our test-kitchen chef, Junichi Takahashi, to tell me anything. He could be homeless, bleeding on the street, and he'd say, "I'm good, Chef, everything is good."

So I asked my mother-in-law, Bente Svendsen, to join us as a sort of grandmother for the staff. She's a psychotherapist by training, and her job now is to make sure everyone feels settled and comfortable. Anything people tell her is confidential, but if she notices patterns among the staff—positive or negative—she lets me know how we might make improvements or adjustments.

None of it has been simple or straightforward. We've got all these twenty-somethings, who all react and adapt differently to every situation. We have to find a way of navigating a whirlpool of different upbringings and cultures and opinions and ways of being. Language is a challenge. It's led to many, many, many, many fuck-ups and misunderstandings. I will say something to the Austrian chef, who goes upstairs and tells his assistant from Malaysia, who then tries to explain it to a German *stagiaire*. Twenty percent of the information is lost with each new translation. Hours later, I see the result and I think, *What is this?*

If our staff were entirely composed of English-speaking Danes, the kitchen would run closer to a perfect machine, but we'd also lose so much. Scandinavians are, for the most part, very open-minded, but they're also incredibly similar. We'd quickly find ourselves thinking and acting the same. We'd fall into old paradigms. Multiculturalism is difficult. It will continue to be difficult. Nothing good comes easily. Growing a tolerant, empathetic culture doesn't happen simply by mixing people from other cultures. Everyone must put in the effort to accept and appreciate that you and the person next to you will never be exactly the same. People from countries like Denmark and the United States often demand that immigrants make an effort to assimilate. But it works both ways. As a host, you have to make it a little bit easier for newcomers.

I can say from experience that the rewards are worth the effort, but the work never ends. I look at my father, a Muslim guy from southern Europe. He spent decades in Denmark, living among Danes, raising a family. He heard many times, "I don't mean you, but all these other Muslims…"

Prejudices are hard to overcome. All we can do is continue to work at it, one person at a time.

Years ago, we began talking about moving Noma out of its original home and into a new space. As these talks unfolded, I would try to envision this new restaurant, and I had this recurring fear that we'd be six months in and I'd look around and we'd be doing exactly the same thing we were doing in the old space.

We've become very good at what we do. We don't have to explain things to our guests; there's a real culture coming to life that understands this place. We've developed an aesthetic that's been adapted throughout the region. But what would be the point of resting on those laurels? If we're not going to push, we might as well stop.

We felt that we needed to go somewhere, to challenge ourselves not to do what we do back home. We wanted to feel what it was like to be in a truly unfamiliar place and to open ourselves up completely to new ways of doing things, so we began planning these extended pop-ups. For the past three years, the entire restaurant staff has spent as much as half the year in a different part of the world.

Our first stint was in Japan. I sent a team ahead of me to start researching and developing new dishes. When I arrived a few weeks later, they had made these dishes that were almost exactly like the ones we made back home, but with Japanese ingredients. I was very critical of them, because exactly what I had been afraid of happening had happened. It takes mental discipline to say, "We're not going to go there." We have to avoid what we know works.

Next up was Sydney, Australia, which is about as far away from Copenhagen as you can get. One of the main reasons we wanted to go there was to see what we could of Aboriginal foodways, and the ingredients first discovered and utilized by Australia's native people: fruits, insects, roots, bushes, things from the ocean.

Over these last few years, we've trained ourselves to embrace the unfamiliar. You have to be okay with being surprised or uncomfortable or ignorant. Otherwise, what's the point of going anywhere? I hate when people come to Denmark and complain, "It's so cold here." Where did you think you were going when you booked your flight? Unfortunately, it's a very common attitude, especially when it comes to food. People just want what they're used to.

I hate to break it to you, but travel requires work, too. When you enter someone's country or home, it's not entirely up to them to help you understand everything. You have to make the effort to understand the culture, including the ways people eat. Read books and papers. Speak to people. Our most recent pop-up was in Tulum, Mexico. We have quite a few friends in Mexico, and we've spent a lot of time there, but we still did lots of reading about Mexican history and cuisine before we arrived.

You have to approach things you don't know with respect and openness. You have to really meet people, go to them, ask them to guide and teach you. We're not perfect, but I think we've done right by the local community wherever we've traveled. We study hard. We don't go to places to take their ideas—we're there for a fleeting moment to expose ourselves to other ways of life and to change our own mind-sets. We pay taxes and put money back into the countries we visit. We try to be more than fair in the amount we pay for ingredients. But everything has consequences. In Mexico, we offered to pay 25 pesos per kilo for corn—usually it's 6 pesos—but people from the local corn syndicate told us, "You can't do this. It's going to disrupt the whole market."

That's the other thing. We have to accept that we'll never fully comprehend the places we visit. We might have a firm grasp on the science of nixtamalization, but nothing can compare to decades of working masa with your hands, breathing in its aroma every day, living on it. Nothing you read can ever give you that sort of mastery, and unless you're willing to change your life completely and permanently, you shouldn't chase that. For us, traveling is about learning from people and seeing things that will inspire us to go back home and cook again.

There is, of course, a small but vocal contingent that sees what we're doing and says, "What are you doing here? You're not Mexican (or Japanese or Australian). You can't cook here." That's a terrible attitude, and I think it reflects some of the more dangerous directions in which the modern world is heading. The day we can't travel and move and learn from each other is the day we all turn into crazy nationalists.

Let's give each other a little bit more room to make mistakes. I'm not talking about deep-rooted, immoral, racist mistakes. I mean well-intentioned errors. Sometimes, when you're from a different part of the world, you say the wrong thing because you don't know any better. That's part of learning, and I don't want to discourage it. I truly believe that leaving your comfort zone and coming into contact with other parts of the world is a must, especially for young cooks. When you learn about others, you learn about yourself. Traveling, migrating, learning, and sharing lift us all up.

Simmering corn in a lye solution enhances its flavor and nutritional value to humans.

# Leaves Make Things Steamy

## Aralyn Beaumont

For all the superficial variations that appear to differentiate the culinary traditions of earth, humans have a remarkable tendency to latch onto the same ideas. For more than twenty thousand years, people everywhere have been wrapping food in leaves and cooking it by a wide range of methods, from submerging the packages in boiling water to smothering them in hot mounds of dirt to steaming them in large cauldrons or earthen ovens. The leaves provide protection from direct heat, dirt, and water. They also trap steam—creating a moist cooking environment—and imbue food with their aroma and flavor.

Any hardy, edible leaf is fair game: bamboo, cherry, pumpkin, grape, cabbage, lotus, pandan, palm, oak, taro, banana, and corn husks. Some leaves have more utility than others; for instance, papaya leaves contain an enzyme called papain, which tenderizes meat. Most often, we unwrap the leaves and eat the cooked contents, as with corn husk–wrapped tamales and lotus leaf–wrapped *lo mai gai*. Sometimes we eat the leaves with the contents inside. Think of grape leaf–wrapped dolmas, cabbage rolls, and *sakura mochi*—delightful pink rice cakes ensconced in pickled cherry leaves one finds in Japan.

Wrapping food in leaves or husks can also help with portability. In the Americas, for instance, the tamale is ubiquitous, beloved because they're so easily transported across both physical and cultural distances. They're usually wrapped in corn husks, except

Wrapping food in leaves is a technique attributed to the people of basically everywhere.

*Cochinita pibil*

*Corn-husk tamale*

*Bánh ít nhan dua*

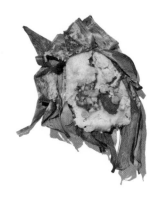

*Zong zi*

Suman

Lo mai gai

Banana-leaf tamale

Mok pla

Mok pla

Sakura mochi

when they're wrapped in banana leaves, as in Oaxaca, the Yucatán, and much of South America. In the Mississippi Delta, they're "hot tamales"—simmered rather than steamed, sometimes smothered in chili and cheese, and usually made with cornmeal instead of masa.

All over the planet, we humans use larger leaves or palm fronds to cover big hunks of meat or even whole animals before burying them underground with hot coals, as with *kalua* pigs or *hāngi* in New Zealand. The principle is the same with clambakes cooked under seaweed or even oyster roasts in the American South, where wet burlap sacks perform the job of leaves. And of course, cooking with leaves is a cousin to the practice of cooking *en papillote*, where food is bundled in parchment paper packets and steamed in the oven.

Cooking in leaves is one of humanity's simplest and most elegant culinary ideas. Its ubiquity unites us. The myriad ways we adapt the same basic principle is what makes food interesting.

## Foods cooked in leaves, organized by leaf

**Arrowroot**
Bánh chung (Vietnam)

**Avocado**
Barbacoa (Mexico)
Sea bass (Mexico)
Tamales (Mexico)

**Bamboo**
Chimaki (Japan)
Fish (Southeast Asia)
Sasaame (Japan)
Zong zi (China)

**Banana**
Amok (Cambodia)
Bánh bot loc la (Vietnam)
Bánh ít nhan dua (Vietnam)
Bánh tét (Vietnam)
Botok (Indonesia)
Cha lua (Vietnam)
Chimaki (Japan)
Cochinita pibil (Yucatán)
Entula, katunkuma (Uganda)
Fish (Indonesia)
Hallaca (Venezuela)
Hor mok (Thailand)
Juanes (Peru)
Kenkey (West Africa)
Khao niao sangkhaya
   (Thailand)
Khao tom mad (Thailand,
   Laos)
Lampong pisang (Indonesia)
Lemper ayam (Indonesia)
Luwombo (Uganda)
Matoke n'yama (Uganda)
Moi moi elewe (Nigeria)
Mok nor mai (Laos)
Mok pla (Vietnam)
Nakati, nakasuga, enderema
   (Uganda)
Otak-otak (Indonesia,
   Malaysia, Singapore)
Pepes ikan (Indonesia)
Pepesan (Java)
Pescado tikin-xic (Yucatán)
Puto (Philippines)

Tamales (Mexico)
Ubai (Papua New Guinea)
Vakalolo (Fiji)

**Cabbage**
Sarma (Turkey)
Steamed cabbage rolls (China,
   Eastern Europe)

**Cherry Blossom**
Sakura mochi (Japan)

**Coconut**
Ketupat (Indonesia, Malaysia )
Otak-otak (Indonesia,
   Singapore)
Suman sa ibus (Philippines)

**Corn husk**
Bollos (Colombia)
Cabanga (Panama)
Chapanas (Peru)
Chumales (Ecuador)
Envueltos de mazorca
   (Colombia)
Humitas (Argentina,
   Bolivia, Chile, Ecuador,
   Paraguay, Peru)
Kenkey (West Africa)
Nacatamal (Nicaragua)
Pamonha (Amazonia)
Tamales (Mexico)

**Canna**
Tamales, quimbolitos
   (Ecuador)

**Fig**
Lavraki stin schara (Greece)

**Grape**
Dolmas (Greece)
Fish (Mediterranean)
Koupepia (Cyprus)
Sarma (Mexico)

**Hoja Santa (Mexican pepperleaf)**
Fish (Mexico)
Tamales (Mexico)

**Lemon**
Polpette con foglie di limone
   (Sicily)

**Lotus**
Beggar's chicken (China)
Lo mai gai (China)

**Maguey**
Barbacoa (Mexico)

**Oak**
Kashiwa mochi (Japan)

**Palm**
Khanom tan (Thailand)
Suman (Philippines)

**Pandan**
Khanom tako (Thailand)

**Papaya**
Meat (Pacific Islands)

**Pumpkin**
Vegetables (Uganda)

**Reed leaves**
Chimaki (Japan)
Zong zi (China)

**Swiss chard**
Rice and minced meat
   (Lebanon and Syria)
Rollos de cordero y acelgas
   (Spain)
Sarma (Turkey)

**Taro**
Laulau pork (United States)
Lu pulu (Tonga)
Palusami (Samoa)
Taro pudding (Solomon
   Islands)

**Ulu**
Palusami (Samoa)

# Food Is a Gateway

Bini Pradhan, Heena Patel, and Isabel Caudillo

The path for many immigrants includes at least a stopover in the food industry. Restaurant or farming jobs are often the only ones available to people with a limited grasp of the local language or culture. But for many immigrant entrepreneurs, food is not only a means of making a living, but also a way of preserving their cultural identity. They contribute to their local economy and community by cooking and selling food that is meaningful to them. Cuisine is built this way, with immigrants arriving in new places and introducing and exchanging ingredients, flavors, and techniques.

San Francisco is home to as many as three hundred thousand immigrants, many of whom identify as entrepreneurs. But due to prohibitively expensive real estate and a dramatically changing economy, it may be one of the most unrealistic cities in America to sustain a small, independent business, especially in the restaurant industry. Over the last couple of decades, nonprofit organizations have stepped up to provide support to small businesses in various industries. La Cocina is an incubator kitchen in the Mission neighborhood of San Francisco that serves low-income entrepreneurs, focusing primarily on helping female immigrants start their own food businesses.

The organization provides commercial kitchen space, training, and marketing opportunities for chefs and food purveyors to create and nurture restaurant concepts, develop menus, and acquire the skills to run a successful business. Since it first opened in 2005, La Cocina has helped launch more than fifty businesses, many of which have transitioned from members of the program to self-sufficient restaurants. Here you'll meet three La Cocina entrepreneurs.

Bini Pradhan is the daughter of a chef to the royal Nepalese family who moved to the United States in search of new opportunities. Now she's selling her *momos*—steamed Nepalese dumplings—out of Bini's Kitchen, which has three food stands in San Francisco and a brick-and-mortar restaurant in the works.

Heena Patel left Mumbai for London in her early twenties to get married. After struggling to adjust to English life, she got a US business visa and moved to California with her husband and children. In California, she learned to speak English and gathered the confidence to join La Cocina and launch her own food business, Rasoi Indian Kitchen.

Before joining La Cocina, Isabel Caudillo was serving food from her house. The more successful she grew, the riskier her hush-hush operation became, so when she heard about La Cocina, she jumped at the opportunity to become a legitimate business. Her restaurant, El Buen Comer, has been met with critical acclaim since it opened in 2017.

These three women each have radically different experiences as immigrant entrepreneurs, and yet, they will ring surprisingly familiar to millions of small-business owners around the world. Immigrant or not, running a restaurant is a labor of love.

## Bini Pradhan
### As told to Joell Hallowell

First, you must try my *momos*. I want everybody to know that these are the best *momos* anywhere in the world. If that could be the title of my story, "Best Momos Ever," that would be my dream. My visions are so big. I want to do so many important things, and I think my dumplings will make it possible.

Cooking was my fate—it was written. My mother was a royal chef in the sixties in Kathmandu, Nepal. It's a big city, beautiful, surrounded by the Himalayas. We were brought up in a very positive, very secure, upscale neighborhood. We were an upper-class family, with three children: my elder brother, my sister in the middle, and me, the youngest. We went to one of the best schools and had all we could ask for. We traveled a lot and took many vacations. We came to the United

States quite often because my dad was an aeronautical engineer and traveled back and forth for his work.

My dad went to college in India and did his engineering degree in France, but he came back home because he always loved Nepal. He met my mom at a social gathering. That's how they fell in love. It was a love marriage, but it was not permitted, because my dad is Newar and my mom is Brahman. They are both at the top of their two castes, but every culture has its taboos, and Dad's family had their own ideas about who should be allowed to marry. It was tough for my parents, but since my dad was educated, he didn't need to rely on his family and he went against his parents. They disowned him from the family, but my dad fought for my mom.

My parents were strict, and we were brought up to respect our elders and to respect food. I was always interested in cooking; I grew up cooking at home with my mom. I used to hold on to her sari and watch what she was doing. I learned which spices to use and all of her secrets. When it came time for college, I went to a hotel management culinary school in India.

Later, my sister married her high school sweetheart, a Nepalese man who went to college in America and wanted to stay there. She came here to be with him, and they became Americans. That's how our family's immigrant story started. In January 2004, I came to San Francisco to be there for my nephew's delivery and then returned to Nepal to my work in food and beverage at the Radisson Hotel. When I came back to the United States for a second visit, I got a very good work offer. I'm a driven woman and I love San Francisco, so I was happy to stay. The city is so beautiful, so diverse. People are so nice. They opened up their hearts to me. I have had so many opportunities here, and I was able to become a US citizen eleven years ago.

I had a good background and a great life in Nepal; I never had any big problems. We were in the upper class of our country, so it was easier for me than most immigrants. I wasn't coming to the United States to escape bad things. My real immigrant challenge only came after I met my now ex-husband.

I met my ex-husband through a mutual friend at the end of 2004. I was working as a cook in San Francisco and he was in the Navy Reserve, going to nursing school in Mississippi. He'd gone to high school in the United States, and when I met him, he did not speak Nepali perfectly. When we got married, I moved to Mississippi to be with him.

I had never seen a place like Mississippi. I had never been to a Waffle House. We would walk into this place and people would stare—I felt like I was being scraped by their eyes. They would say things like, "You little poor thing." And I'm wondering, *What poor thing? I am a poor thing?* They'd say, "You are pretty and so small. You are like a doll." People's eyes would creep from my hair to my toes. I hadn't felt foreign in San Francisco. In San Francisco, almost everybody was born somewhere else. They came there, it was a good life, and they stayed there. We are all immigrants here—that's the thing.

Once I moved to Mississippi, the abuse started. My husband was an alcoholic and he sexually, physically, and mentally abused me for nine years. Every minute, I had to wonder what was going to be next. He did not want me to pray to certain gods, he did not allow me to use the phone or make friends. He isolated me completely.

One of the worst incidents—out of thousands—was the time he threw beef in my face. The Nepalese don't eat beef, but for my husband, I had gone against my beliefs and cooked it for him. When he threw it at me, he said, "You are nothing." That was how I always felt: *I am nothing, I am very heavy for this earth.*

In the beginning, I thought it was how he showed his love, his affection. I'm someone who studied abroad. I was a confident woman who had been working high up in the food and beverage industry in a renowned hotel. But when I started living with my husband, I became scared just to make a phone call. My voice used to shake. He was always judging me, and if anything went wrong, I was blamed.

I didn't know what abuse was—I'd never seen it. In Nepal, I had been in such a secure environment, I did not know these things happened. I did not dare tell my parents. Even my sister didn't know. I didn't call her for two years because my husband wouldn't allow it. Everything my husband said or did to me, I kept to myself.

The abuse became even more severe after my son was born. I couldn't breast-feed my little one because the milk was not coming. The stress started weighing more and more. One day, my sister was finally able to reach me by phone. It was a bad time. Either I would have killed my husband or he would have killed me. I soon moved to a shelter in Turlock, California, and then we came back to my sister's house in San Francisco. After a few months, I started cooking again.

My sister runs a day care in San Francisco, and one of her clients knew that I was a very good cook. He ordered some food from me and became my first client. That's how I started—slowly, slowly, slowly, from one person to another by word of mouth. As business picked up, my parents came for six months to help me get started. My mom helped cook and put the food in bags; even my dad helped me to chop the vegetables. My brother-in-law made a website for me. I used to go all over the city with grocery bags full of my food. I put my son in the car full of bags and I drove all over the place dropping off dinners. We had all his educational stuff with us, and he would sleep in the car. I used to park in driveways to change his diaper. At first, I cooked at my sister's house, and then I moved to the apartment where I am now. After eight months, I had about one hundred fifty clients.

Everybody used to ask me, "Are you from La Cocina?" Over and over people asked me, and I'm wondering, *What is La Cocina?* Finally, one of my sister's clients told me that it was a place to learn and get help starting a business, and that I should apply. He thought I'd be a good fit. I came for an orientation, and the kitchen was full of people. I never thought I was going to get in.

My brother-in-law and my sister came with me to the interview. After the mental abuse I had gone through, I had no confidence left. The people at La Cocina asked me about my business plan and I told them straight that I was not in a condition to do that for myself. My brother-in-law answered all the business plan questions. But when it came to the food, I know how to cook. They wanted to try my food. About ten people from La Cocina sat and ate my food. The first thing they tried were my *momos*, and they loved them. I got a call later saying I was in. It's amazing, right? I was looking for a place to help me get started, and there it was.

La Cocina has become a second home for me and for my son. I don't have words to express my gratitude. I can never repay this organization. The people who work here have helped me so much. I had skills, I know, but this is the place that showed me the way to enhance what qualities I have and polish them. Suddenly, I had a place that was secure, safe—a haven to be who I am.

My food is comfort food, but not heavy—it's healthy and clean. My clients say that my vegetarian *momos* are the best dumplings they've ever tasted. In Nepal, the food is mostly vegetarian. We don't eat meat in an everyday way—meat is only for feasts. There is a misconception about Nepalese food that it's the same as Indian food, but all the spices are very different. We have different spices even for our chai tea. I get the ingredients from Nepal and then I sun-dry and grind them here. My brother-in-law often goes to Nepal—he's opened a solar company that helps remote villages—and I ask him to bring me specific spices. He brings packets to me every six months. It's difficult to import. You have to label it just right and tell customs exactly what it is.

Even very young kids love my food. At my sister's day care, the small, small kids can each eat twenty-five *momos*. Whenever I visit, the kids start chanting: "*Momos! Momos!*" Some of their parents have become my clients.

It's now five years that I've been with La Cocina. I have to graduate one day, of course. I have a big production going on. I do a lot of catering—private parties and formal, sit-down weddings. Lots of things are happening. Right now, I'm cooking about twenty-eight thousand of these little *momos*, a thousand pounds of rice, and a thousand pounds of chicken every week. I do farmers' markets in Sausalito and at the Ferry

Building on Saturdays. I sell food at Off the Grid at Fort Mason. I even have a very small kiosk restaurant right outside the Montgomery BART station. I have big goals. I'd like to do music festivals and more farmers' markets. Eventually, I want to have a place where people can come and sit—a few tables, with a small kitchen up front. I want transparency, where people can watch me make *momos*. But my big goal is to have hundreds of small kiosks all over the United States. My vision is to take my *momos* everywhere.

When I cook, I think something passes from my heart to my employees to the food and to the person who eats. When someone takes the first bite, I see that smile and it makes my day. It's the love response. I say my cooking is food for the soul, because I cook it from my soul and I hope it feeds the soul of whoever eats it. It's important for the cook to think about this. I'll give you an example.

When you have a fight with your partner in the morning, you cook with that same mentality. When you cook when you're happy, you can taste a big difference. I tell my employees, "If you're angry, just go for a break and yell or take a walk around. When you are cooking my food, don't be angry."

I have twelve employees. Most of them are Tibetan and Nepalese. It's a lot of responsibility, but I feel blessed. It's why I have to be on top of everything and make myself stable. Once I'm stable, then I can look after others better. I'm grateful that the city of San Francisco has increased the minimum hourly rate for employees. Of course, I'm a businesswoman and I'm struggling, but we all work hard and we should be paid well for our hard work. My employees are the best. I take care of them, and they take care of me.

I'm grateful that I am educated and that I could speak English before I came to America. Now I want to lift up immigrants here who don't have the skills or support they need. Many are not educated. I have a few women with me who have been abused, but I need to find a platform to help these women. I need to be successful so that I can help them better.

Besides being a successful chef, my other big goal, which I'm working on, is to do something for women who have gone through domestic violence. Every day I am keeping a little money in an account so eventually I can assist women who have gone through the things I have gone through.

When I look back at the abuse now, I think it's easier to get over the physical abuse, but when it comes to emotional abuse, it's super hard to recover. Once I finally started grabbing for my own ground, I realized I had to speak up. There are people who are scared to death to come out about similar experiences, but I hope they will be able to reach out to me. Women, especially immigrant women, don't speak up enough. It's fear. Fear is very, very weird stuff that makes you unstable. You freeze.

Right now, my employees are all immigrants, and they are scared to death of the new politics in America. Whatever is going on in the news, they come to me scared. And the politics have impacted my business as well. People are not spending as much as they did. Even my American-born customers are scared to spend. They are cutting back and keeping their money, not spending on weddings and extra expenses. They used to eat lunch at a restaurant four or five days a week—now that has been cut down to just once a week. The new politics have impacted all of us.

Next to my bed there is a small temple where I have Lord Ganesha and Goddess Lakshmi. Every morning I meditate there. It keeps me going. I light candles for my parents, candles for my business, candles for people I love. I light candles for my employees. One for each. I talk to my higher power, who's right in front of me. I follow my intuition, and it's like my angels are looking after me.

It's been two and a half years since I left my ex-husband, and I'm working hard to forgive this guy. Not for him, but for me and my son. I was becoming bitter, and I didn't like how that felt. I decided that I will work until the day I am able to forgive him. I go to therapy every week for my soul and for my son. He's a great boy, and I want to be a great mother. When I go home at night, he can see me downstairs parking my car. I'm dead tired, but when I see my son at the window and he says, "Mama, Mama!," his love makes everything melt away.

He's going to be nine this July, and I am in a place now where I can show him how to fish rather than bringing him the fish. One of the reasons I want to do things for other people is to be an example for my son. I'm trying to teach him to respect women. When you have kids, you want to do the right thing. When I work really hard, it's to set an example for my son.

I have a good life with meaning. I feel that I'm here to fulfill a purpose. Until the day I can't, I will keep doing this work. I will never quit. Whatever happens happens for a reason. I understand that. When I got married, God put me in a position to be a part of making my husband successful. He needed me to be his helper, and now he's a nurse. I'm not taking credit for that—I'm just saying that I was with him for a purpose.

After that purpose, this new purpose came, and with this purpose, I'm helping others. And if I want to help my community, then I need to be honest so that people can see me. I'm not scared to talk about the abuse, because maybe that's going to help people. For example, I'm talking to you, so my story will go somewhere, right? People will read this and they'll think, *She is an immigrant, she's surviving, she's successful, and she's a helper.*

## Heena Patel
### As told to Aralyn Beaumont

I grew up splitting my time between Mumbai and Ahmedabad, in the western part of India, where all of my extended family lives. Ahmedabad is in Gujarat, a pretty big state, where the majority of the population is vegetarian, because of the religion. I've realized now that my whole cuisine growing up was vegan.

Monday through Saturday, my mom cooked two times a day: in the morning for a full lunch, and at nighttime when we'd eat something lighter. A typical menu at home included rice, roti, pickles, and two types of vegetables—one green and one legume, to get our protein.

My grandmother and my mom would cook outside. They'd build up a big flame and I could see them cooking from the house. Usually my grandfather would be working in the field and by twelve or one o'clock, everything would be cooked and he'd sit down to eat. Everything they made was from what they'd grown. My grandmother would make fresh mango chutney by hand right on the farm.

She never touched an onion with a knife. She'd squeeze the juice out by hand—it was so delicious. It doesn't taste the same when you cut it with a knife. Those are the details I remember. I try to do the same now, because I see how it tasted so good with the simplest ingredients they used—just turmeric, salt, chilies, cilantro, no garam masala or anything. Just simple okra tasted so good. It's something I try to recall from my memory and re-create.

Our family was big, and food was always around me. Weddings are a very big deal in India—we celebrate for four or five days. We'd put up a tent outside and cook for two to three days. When I was seven or eight, I started staying up late to see how they cooked. They'd be

cooking overnight because they had to make enough food to feed four to five hundred people. They made it look so easy, cooking for that many people. I got so fascinated by the big pots and cooking such a large volume.

The first thing I cooked myself was a disaster. I'd been asked to cook potato *sabzi* for dinner—just a dry, roasted potato, something very plain to accompany chapati, but I couldn't even do that. I forgot to soak my potatoes in water so they wouldn't turn black. I put the whole thing together and the oil went everywhere. My mom said, "That's it, you're not cooking anymore." That was my first cooking experience. I have four sisters, so my mom had no patience with us girls. Instead of teaching us to cook, she would always say, "Let me just do it and get it done."

———

When we were in Mumbai, my family all lived together in a little apartment outside of the city. It wasn't comfortable, but Mumbai is very tight and there are a lot of people, so it was exciting, too.

Mumbai is a lot like San Francisco, more metropolitan and with different regional food. It was all Indian, but it made my horizon wider. I had a neighbor upstairs—we called her *kaki*, which means "auntie"—and when I was around fifteen or sixteen, I used to go upstairs and watch her cook. Her cooking was so different from my mom's. She would cook this one item I'm still trying to re-create here. It's called *patoli*. It's similar to tamales. She made a batter out of rice flour and coconut, with ginger and chilies, and put it in the middle of two leaves and steamed it. It's served with peanut oil for dipping. It's vegan and absolutely delicious. I can't wait to go back and ask her to make it. She's old now, but she keeps in touch with my parents.

Our home was a very tight space compared to our home in Gujarat. In Gujarat, there are big houses and farms. In Mumbai, we were living in a two-bedroom apartment, as a middle-class family. Everything we had, we had to share. Nobody in the building closed their doors, so you always smelled what everyone was cooking. Next door there was a Jain family. They all were vegetarian, but they also didn't eat potatoes because of their religion. They made *khakhra*—it's a very crisp, very thin cracker made with wheat flour, and you just put a little bit of spice on top. They ate it for breakfast and at night. Every time we went over there, they'd make stacks of it. There were four ladies in the house and many children. I was friends with one of the daughters. I'd always sneak into the house to eat *khakhra*.

When I was twenty years old, my dad asked me, "Do you want to study more?" I told him no, so he said, "Then you're getting married." I said okay—I never questioned it. I got married as soon as I graduated.

I got married in London. My father's sister was already there, as was my older sister—she married an Indian guy who had already settled in London. I never questioned what I was told to do and never thought about what I wanted. I was so naive then. I never even considered what I wanted to do. Before I left, my dad had already arranged for me to meet a few suitors. My husband was the fifth one. It was a lot of fun to see guys and say no. I had a good time.

My husband and I got engaged in two weeks. I moved to London in November and our engagement happened in December, then I went back to India for a year. When I came back to London the following December, we had our Hindu wedding.

I didn't know how to speak English, but even in London, I could survive because we spoke Gujarati with the family. I lived with my in-laws, and I could get by without speaking English. When I came to America, I became more exposed through owning a business, but in London, I didn't realize the urgency of speaking English because everybody spoke Gujarati. I didn't have any friends there. It's hard to make friends if you can't speak, right? I was lonely in that sense.

I was in London for five years. I had started working, but I got pregnant straight away and I had a baby within one year, so I stayed home with my mother-in-law. I learned to cook from my mother-in-law. She had gotten married in India before moving to Kampala, the capital of Uganda. She introduced me to vegetables I had never used in India.

My in-laws lived in Africa for fifteen years before moving to London. I think every time a family migrates, they kind of adapt. They have to. When they grow up with one thing and try to re-create it in a new place that might not have the same ingredients, they have to change. My mother-in-law grew up in Mumbai, but she was Gujarati. She adapted to the ingredients available in Africa and tried to re-create what she grew up eating in Mumbai.

My mother-in-law likes to use plantains and peanuts and coconut in a vegetable *sabzi*, while my mom likes to use lots of chilies. My in-laws don't like spicy, but my mom loves it. She starts with two or three types of chilies and builds up—she gets excited when you get a bite of chili.

My mother-in-law taught me about patience and slowing down while cooking, and my mom taught me about taste. Most of the items I cook now are based on how I remember the taste of their foods. I try to bring the same taste with different ingredients, the ingredients that I'm surrounded by. I use a lot of mushrooms—I love how mushrooms have pores and absorb the flavor—but my mom never did. In India, they don't eat mushrooms because it's something they relate with the street, because people see them growing close to the gutter. My mom doesn't think it's a good food to eat; they don't understand you can make it edible.

Rasoi, the name of my business, means "kitchen," or the process of cooking. My *rasoi*, my process of cooking, was influenced by seeing all these moms cooking, by staying with them and watching how they did it. I know when I do the same thing as them, it will taste different because we all end up doing things slightly different and use different amounts of the same things.

We came to America in 1992 on a business visa. We were not happy in London. I was trying to adjust to London and marriage and pregnancy and having a baby—everything was happening at the same time, and because I was just trying to adjust, I didn't get a chance to enjoy the city or relax.

We were so young. My husband wasn't happy with his job and we were living with my in-laws, because as a young family it was impossible to settle down on our own in London. I was open to coming to America and seeing how it was different.

My brother-in-law was already living in Sausalito, north of San Francisco, and he said, "Why don't you come here and check it out? If you like it, I will help you settle here." So it's something we took a chance on. We didn't know how it was going to go, but we had two years with the business visa to decide. If it didn't work out, we could go back. At the time, if you said you wanted to open a business, they'd give you a visa for two years. All you had to do was prove you had a business before the visa expired.

When I came to California, my cooking became more experimental. My children would expose me to what they'd see at school. They always wanted to eat lasagna and pasta, so I was interested in cooking that and learning about different cuisines. The lasagna I make uses paneer instead of Italian cheese. I make the paneer myself. I try to create the foods of other cuisines using the flavors of India.

My daughter used to say, "Mom, even if you cook tacos, it tastes like Indian food."

I always want to know more. I don't eat fish, so I don't need to know how to cook fish or stuff it, but I want to know the technique and use that on my produce. I want to know about barbecue so I can learn about overcooking and undercooking my produce and how to get good flavor. Different cuisines here expose me to so many techniques. I had never had Chinese or Thai food before I came here, and I was so happy because they're so spicy and so delicious, with so much flavor, and so different from Indian food. Thai food became my go-to food here.

When we first arrived, we didn't have as many ingredients as in London, and we had to go to Berkeley for my Indian supplies. Now there are so many Indian stores everywhere, but it was a big thing back then to go to Berkeley to eat Indian food and go to Vik's Chaat. They were selling Mumbai street food in the back of a store. It tasted so close to what I had growing up, I made an excuse to go every weekend.

I always said to my husband, "Let's go shopping," and he'd say, "But I don't need anything." But I'd still go.

I felt very connected with Mumbai when I was eating at Vik's Chaat. At the time, they only had a few seats, and you had to wait until a table was empty, so everybody stood over you until you finished eating. It's typical of India.

We'd also go to the farmers' market in San Rafael, which is so beautiful—it's very big and very spacious and the weather is so nice and it's next to a garden. When she saw it, my mom said, "This is like Mumbai, this is like back home," because we'd always go out and buy our produce from the street and all the farmers would be there. In San Rafael, we'd buy a pastry and push my daughter in her pushcart and enjoy the atmosphere. As soon as the farmers would see I was Indian, they'd say, "You want *methi*? Fenugreek?" Even the farmers knew what Indians buy. It was nice.

We all eat different food—it's what makes me different—but it is also a way for me to connect with people. I can speak with the flavors I create and the ingredients I use—that gives me a voice. If it's bold or spicy, that's because I am. I'm not going to back down if somebody says it's too spicy. That's something I don't want to change. I want to keep my memory of my food.

My husband and I opened a liquor store and a flower store in San Rafael, in Marin County—I did the flower store and my husband did the liquor store.

I got my green card and labor certificate in 2000 through a wurst house that sold sandwiches next to my liquor store. When they opened a second location, they were looking for a night manager for that restaurant. The owner said, "Heena, I know you're busy, but I really like you and I wish you could take this job." I told them I could do it and closed my flower store. That experience taught me so much about how restaurants work, what it takes, and how much money goes into it. Working there gave me firsthand experience in the business. It planted the seed.

The thing is, look, I had a liquor store and I never used to drink. I worked at the wurst house but I don't eat meat. I was surrounded by items I don't indulge in. I really wanted to see what it felt like to do the stuff I enjoy. I feel like all my life I did what I was told, but I never asked for anything. I was interested in cooking, but there wasn't time. Raising children here with the businesses was really hard. Cooking takes so much of you. I waited until we got rid of the businesses, then

I said, O*kay, now I really want to do this. I'm getting old, I don't want to feel like I didn't give it a try.*

My daughter's friend had started business school and I asked her how I could go about writing a business plan. She said we should try this nonprofit organization called La Cocina. I really liked their mission of helping immigrant women start businesses. I felt like they were talking to me directly.

I didn't have resources: no money or knowledge of how to start cooking professionally. I only knew how to cook, but that's not good enough to start a business. It takes a lot—only 20 percent of the business is food. The other time is spent on marketing and writing recipes and focusing on how to keep the money flowing. That's where La Cocina comes in.

I remember my daughter's friend saying, "Don't get upset, Auntie, if they don't accept you, because it's very competitive." We came for the orientation and I brought my food. I brought five or six different items, mostly the food I'm proud of making, like *vada pav, pav bhaji*—Mumbai street food, very tasty small bites. I didn't know how much they'd want to eat, so I brought a lot of food, and they really liked it. There were like sixty or seventy applicants, and I think four were selected.

When I started with La Cocina, I thought I knew everything and had everything sorted out. But running this business the last couple of years, I've realized that sometimes what I want to cook is not profitable. I don't want to make certain food, because I feel like it's too simple—I don't understand why people would go out to eat something so easy to make—and sometimes I don't want to make certain food because it's too common. But I've had to change the menu and learn how to cook chicken, because it's the most requested item.

I sell meat now because it seemed like good business sense—it's as simple as that. I'm still debating it, though. If I open my own space, I may not do it. I may keep it all vegetarian, all vegan. I don't see meat as bad, and I feel like I know how to cook good meat dishes, so why not? And I get excited to cook with new stuff, like the lamb meatballs. I always make my sauces beforehand and taste and adjust the seasoning before I put the meat in. My husband eats meat. He is happy to be a guinea pig, so he's always ready and he always has an opinion. He's the biggest fan of my food.

My whole family is involved. It takes all of them. My children help me with the e-mails, marketing, and Instagram and Twitter. I'm constantly not learning fast enough for them. I may be wrong grammatically, so they log on to Instagram and change the captions.

Having this business gives me more strength and more confidence. I want to be so different and so loud. I want to prove that even if I migrated, even if I'm from India, it doesn't make me bad. I feel like I never had confidence growing up in India with so many sisters. I've always been told to calm down—not to have a voice.

Once, when I had the flower store, I got this phone call. I didn't yet know how to write down phone numbers, because in England the format is different. The customer on the phone got so upset with me, they said, "Why the F did you open a business if you don't even know how to write the phone number? Go back to your country."

I should have slammed the phone down on that person, but it was such a shock to hear that. How can someone say that, just because I didn't know how to write a phone number? We saw more racism in London than here, but we just accepted that as something you see when you leave your country. In London, I was still very young. As you get older, because you know you haven't done anything wrong, you fight back. I see racism like that, and it makes me stronger.

I think it comes with confidence, and of course, education helps. I want my children to know how to be good people. And I worry. I'm very worried about my son having facial hair, even if he has US citizenship. Ignorant people take him for a Muslim, as if we all look like one type of person, so when he travels for school, I worry. But I want him to be himself, he's such a proud Indian boy. I will never say, "Get rid of the facial hair." I want my children to know truly who they are and to treat people as human beings. It's very important for me to be true to myself so they can feel like they can fight when they see racism, too.

My food tells the story of my migration. I believe eating different food makes us so much richer. It's so much more interesting than having the same type of food. I feel frustrated when people ask for the same dish they're used to seeing. I want to show them what I know. *Pav bhaji*—a spicy red mash made from leftover vegetables, like tomatoes, cauliflower, green beans, and *chaat masala* that's served with a soft bread roll—is my favorite food from growing up in Mumbai. I want everyone to experience the same excitement that I remember from eating it. It's difficult, because I'm introducing new items.

I treat it like a challenge: I sell my *pav bhaji* with an egg as a brunch at the Ferry Building farmers' market on Saturdays. Americans can relate to that. They see it and think, *Okay, I can eat this like a sandwich.* I don't mind doing that because I want people to try it. I want people to try different flavors, so I'll put it in something they know and understand.

When I go to India now I feel like an outsider. I think being in San Francisco without family members has shaped me a lot. In a sense, it's only my husband and me here. His brother-in-law went back to London, so now we're alone. That's made us closer, made us very tight. We also rely more on our communities, like La Cocina and the neighbors with the wurst house who helped me get my green card. Those kinds of people are my family now, as good as my parents, because I spend so much time with them.

I didn't go back to India for sixteen years, while we had the businesses in San Rafael. Now I go more often, and my children are big enough to come, too. I thought my children would be very uncomfortable when I brought them to India, because it's a different type of place with different bathrooms. They were so open about it, it made me feel less pressured. My son was eight years old at the time, and he said, "Mom, if you want to come back to India, I can live here."

I'm going again next month, because my parents are getting old and they're getting more fragile and more emotional, so I want to spend more time with them. I'm very excited to go back and eat more food. I learn through experience, and now the cuisine is also changing in India. There's more produce than what I grew up with, like kiwi and broccoli. The world is getting smaller. Now if you go to the India Food Network YouTube channel or watch food shows in Mumbai or India, they're all talking about Mexican cuisine. They're more excited to cook Mexican and Chinese, and I'm just more excited to cook Indian food.

**Isabel Caudillo**
**As told to Paola Vergara**

I immigrated to the United States in 2001 with my husband and three of my children, looking for a better future for my family. We had been living in the Ramos Millán neighborhood of Mexico City, where my husband was a taxi driver and I took care of the children at home. We arrived in Santa Rosa, in Northern California, and stayed with my husband's niece for three months before moving to San Francisco.

When we arrived, the rent seemed really high to us. My husband found work at a cafeteria, and I began babysitting. For a year, I regularly took care of five children.

Friends from Ramos Millán started coming to visit, and of course I'd give them something to eat and invite them to sit down with us. One day I said to them, "I want to help my husband—I want to work." They asked me, "Why don't you sell your food?"

I started to sell food from my home in 2005. I put a big table in the dining room and people would show up and sit right down to eat. Acquaintances we knew from our old neighborhood in Mexico and friends here in the States came together to help me spread the word. I would make rice, or soup with soft pasta, *guisado* (meat cooked in salsa), tortillas, and *agua fresca*, all for seven dollars. That's how I began in our apartment in the Tenderloin.

People told me that I could be fined for selling food out of my house without a license, and I did worry about the legality of it, but it was the only thing I knew I could do. We moved to our current house here on Twenty-Second and Van Ness in the Mission, and I continued to sell my food. All the same people who came to our old house followed us to our new one. During the week I'd sell *guisados*, and Saturday and Sunday I sold appetizers: quesadillas, gorditas, *pambazos*, *migas*, and broth. More people started coming on the weekends, and my children and our nieces would help me out—they'd serve the food, my husband would set out the cheese and cream, and I would toast the quesadillas and gorditas and tacos and serve the broth. My youngest son fought with my nieces, because he would tell me, "Mama, the customers give the girls tips, but I'm the one passing out the plates of food." People would give them three, four, five dollars, and for them it was great.

In 2007, I entered the program at La Cocina, a nonprofit that helps women start food businesses. I learned about La Cocina from my friend Veronica, who joined the program in 2005 and started a restaurant in Marin County called El Huarache Loco. I was watching her little boy at the time, and she told me I should join, too.

La Cocina is difficult to enter. When I applied, I had to take an exam. The director, Caleb, and other people from the program came to my house to taste my cooking, and I did a presentation at La Cocina. It took seven months to start cooking, because they made me write down my recipes and weigh out the food—the rice, toma-

toes, water, everything—all the stuff I always ignored because in my house, I cooked however I wanted to. I always carried all the recipes in my head. If I'm going to make *tinga* or *mole*, I know what goes into it and how much, because it's something I make every day. My *mole* recipe is from my mother. On special occasions, Mom and my sisters would make their special foods, and for my mom that was always red *mole* with chicken and rice.

They also sent me to different restaurants to see prices, how different places were serving their plates, and what they were doing with their food. They would take all of us out for a tour of different restaurants to see what was unique about each one. Even though I don't speak English, they supported me and inspired me. They told me that it didn't matter, as long as I could cook the food.

Even though my children help me, English has been a great

struggle for me. That has been one of the biggest hurdles in my life. It's difficult to communicate with my customers. Sometimes I want to do things by myself, but I can't because of the language barrier. I would love to learn English, but I always return to the same problem: I don't have time to dedicate myself to studying and learning it well. My sons and daughters-in-law and nieces are the ones who help me translate so I can do business with clients and vendors.

When I entered La Cocina, they told me, "You're going to join our program, but you have to stop selling out of the house, because they will fine you." I said, "Okay," and stopped. I started selling food at small functions and a farmers' market in Noe Valley in 2007: *chilaquiles*, *tacos dorados*, enchiladas, tamales, quesadillas, and pozole. The program at La Cocina runs for five to six years—they support you until you can get a loan or some kind of financial support to start a restaurant. They helped me find the space for my restaurant. I told them I wasn't ready yet, especially because of my English, but they told me I could do it. They helped me rent it and decorate it and make the website—they helped with everything. Everyone who works at my restaurant are friends of my children or women I know from La Cocina.

I feel better being able to attend to customers in my own restaurant. My restaurant is my second home, but now I have to pay for many more things as well. And I definitely spend less time at home with my children because of the work. It's so difficult to balance work with my family life, but I do it because I want to be able to give my children as much as possible.

During the first few months, I was very stressed and worried. At the time, I'd been making food for weddings and parties. It's different running a restaurant. I was so afraid. The restaurant is very big and there is so much pressure, because this work has to pay all of the bills. Sometimes in the mornings, when there are very few people here, my kids despair, and I tell them, "While we have enough to pay the employees, and the bills, and the rent, we are fine." They ask me, "Ay, Mama, why did you sign the lease for such a long time?" They could have given it to me for five years instead of seven, but I say, "Well, that's it, what's done is done." A year has passed and there are six more to go. I don't know how the rest of those years will go. But here we are, and after that, who knows. I don't know if I'll keep the restaurant or not after my lease ends.

Sometimes I get nervous because the rent is so high. Even now it's not easy—we're spending so much money on paying employees and all the other costs. We're fine right now, but I'm still making food for events to help pay for the costs here. I tell myself, *I'm going to be here until I can't anymore*, and hopefully it'll go well for us until the lease ends. I'm not making plans. At the end, we'll see if my children say, "Let's keep doing this" or "No, it's over"—it depends on them as well. They've been so compromising. I tell them that in a few years, if they want to do their own thing, if they want to find a better place for the restaurant or take it over, they can do what they want.

I've gone around to various restaurants of my classmates, and they all have different experiences. One of them told me, "I wish I'd never gotten this restaurant. It's so difficult." Another one told me, "You do it, and if you succeed, good, and if not, it doesn't matter." That inspired me. Yes, it has been difficult, but it doesn't matter—I signed the contract and I have to come through.

It's good to try to see what one can do. I see all of the people coming to eat, and they're happy, and that gives me so much joy. Watching the customers come in with requests and return again—it's beautiful.

Here in the Mission neighborhood, there's a lot of Mexican food. I don't know what is different about mine, but I cook everything with love. I'm never mad when I'm cooking.

We have customers who have been with us since we started. There's one person whose wedding I cooked for back when we first started selling food, maybe nine years ago now. She still comes to the farmers' market every week, and sometimes she comes to the restaurant, too. She takes pictures of all the food—I don't know what she does with them.

I am at the restaurant all day, from very early in the morning until ten p.m., but I go home calm. I have my sons and daughters-in-law here helping me. The youngest one helps in the morning and the older ones come to help in the afternoon. My husband is here practically all the time anyway, so we all see each other here. I tell them it's good for them to work here, because at least here we're all together and they're making money, too.

That's my story since coming to this country: I sold my house, joined La Cocina, and now I have the restaurant. That is what we have lived since we arrived.

# Food Changes

## Tony Tan
as told to Rachel Khong

*The first time I meet Tony Tan, it's over a feast he's cooked, course after course of thoughtful Chinese-meets-Australian food: gnocchi made from taro, served with his signature XO sauce; local oysters with a chili sauce, plated alongside a raw fish salad of King George whiting with lemongrass and thinly sliced kumquat; snappy mung bean noodles made sour with black vinegar and his homemade pickled ginger; Hakka-style salt-baked chicken with a bright green ginger-scallion sauce. He sautés a heap of vegetables and seasons them with* kakadu *plums, a local Australian variety that adds a fascinating acidity. There's a crabmeat omelet that he cooks in a wok until the eggs are perfectly, barely set, and serves with a scattering of chilies he's pickled himself but which remind me of the Malaysian chilies you find at hawker food stalls. They're all familiar Chinese Malaysian flavors that surprise me with their thoughtfulness and freshness.*

*Over the next few days, Tony takes me to his favorite Melbourne restaurants: Flower Drum, the illustrious Chinese banquet restaurant that's been part of Melbourne's food scene for forty years, where the service is so good, the waiters draw little ducks out of the hoisin sauce that comes with your Peking duck; and Embla, a wine bar where a snapper carpaccio blows me away. At Flower Drum, he's greeted with a glass of sparkling wine. At Embla, the chef sneaks him a loaf of his house-made bread. Tan is well known in Melbourne's food circles for his passion and enthusiasm, and he is well loved.*

*What Tony and I have in common is that our Chinese families immigrated to Malaysia. From there, we left—to other places. From Kuantan, Malaysia, where his Hainanese family was in the café business, Tony moved to Australia, "ostensibly to finish university." But there, during the "tail end of the hippie era," his life took a very different turn.*

*The beginning of his Australian story is that he fell in with macrobiotic hippies at a vegetarian restaurant called Shakahari that still exists in Melbourne and serves food with a Southeast Asian twist. He was the only Chinese Malaysian working at the restaurant at the time and started by washing dishes on weekends. Then he was asked to make a dish, and he did: coconut cream pie, with a Malaysian twist. He started cooking regularly on Saturdays.*

It was my first time here in Australia and there was nobody to guide me. It was nothing like Malaysia, where nothing was unusual to me. Upstairs at the former Shakahari was the meditation room. On Friday nights, there were all the devotees that would come upstairs and chant. It was an amazing experience. Who would have ever thought that there would be something like this in a restaurant? They were the ones who first got me into smoking dope. I didn't even know what that was like—the Chinese culture is so very traditional. The first time I smoked dope, I was like, *Oh my God!*

I never knew that it was going to be like that. Learning a different culture, learning what it's like to live an alternative lifestyle. Learning what it's like to understand meditation. I became vegetarian. I became macrobiotic. You're very impressionable, you see, because you walk around and everyone is just so cool. Everybody is older and they tell you, "You must not do this, you should only eat brown rice."

There are times when you feel very self-conscious, particularly when you are born in Malaysia. There are obviously Asians in Australia, but there were not as many back then. And also at that time, it was a very racist country. So you try to blend in, but it's not that easy. You look different, you sound different. You start eating brown rice, you start eating lentils. Of course, it took me a while to get used to all that brown rice.

For me, it was just a whole new experience. It was also very scary in the sense that suddenly I'm on my own. I'm supposed to come here, study, and then go home. I lost half my body weight adjusting to eating nothing but grains and proteins from the macrobiotic kingdom. You're allowed to have miso, but you can't have eggs, you can't have cheese. Eventually it was just a little too much, and the owner of the restaurant decided that he had had enough of serving that kind of food, so we were introducing Southeast Asian dishes. Because I grew up in Malaysia, curries were second nature to me. If I don't have curry once a week, I have withdrawal symptoms.

*Tony had been working at Shakahari for several years when the owner decided to sell, and Tony and two other Malaysian friends working at the restaurant joined forces to buy it. The three of them bought Shakahiri for twelve thousand dollars.*

Here I am, just turning twenty, and the owner of a restaurant. It was shocking, but we did it. What we were doing at that time was quite revolutionary. We were doing vegetarian things, things that we'd learned from our experiences in Malaysia, and turning them on their heads. Obviously, we would grind our own roasted peanuts and make that into a sauce. Vegetarian food in its raw state can be very, very boring. You've got to introduce flavors to make it really work. That's what we did. When we got our first write-up, it was so exciting! That's when the restaurant started taking off.

It must have been during the first couple of years when my parents turned around and said, "Because you're not studying, we're not giving you any more money."

I said, "Don't worry, I can look after myself. I have my own restaurant."

And they said, "What? Why did you want a restaurant? It's not becoming. You should be an engineer, you should be a doctor, you should be an accountant. But definitely not work in a kitchen! It's so much hard work."

In Malaysia, my father was known as the restaurant king in town. Both my parents had worked as house cooks. They worked for the British for a long time. They knew what a trifle was, they knew what a scone was. During the British period, they used to run a rest house that was meant for division one officers.

They were not impressed. I didn't fulfill the normal role that was required of so many Asian kids. And of course I didn't tell them about Terry.

*About the time he was buying the restaurant, Tony met an Australian man named Terry. He was a lawyer, a little bit older than Tony. They started to date. I ask if Tony knew that he was gay growing up. "I had an inkling. I didn't go out looking for girls." But he didn't necessarily have the vocabulary for it. In Australia, that changed.*

At that time, it was just like, *Oh my God. These people are gay. What's it like to be gay?* I was discovering my sexuality, because all those years in Malaysia, you're so repressed. You just go to school. You study. That's all you do. If you talk about girls, you go, "Hee hee hee." Anyway, studies got left behind. Sex life took over. Testosterone was just going out of control. By that time, I was already a dope-smoking hippie. Still feeling the pangs of conscience that sort of stuck, but I was too busy discovering myself.

*Tony and Terry decided to move to Sydney to open their own restaurant, called Tatler's Café: Tony would cook and Terry would handle the business side.*

It was in Sydney that I made a name for myself. Either the third or the fourth month into this venture, when we were down to our last thousand dollars, we had our first review. After we got written up, everybody wanted to come in. It just became crazy.

We were open five nights a week and five days a week. On the fifth night we would die from exhaustion. On the sixth night we were making our own breads, starting all over from scratch again. We were also making our own pasta. We would go out to the wholesale market to buy our own vegetables and all that stuff. It was fun, but it was scary.

Terry and I started fighting, because I refused to take shortcuts. At the end of the day, it was my reputation. That's how you succeed. Ultimately we had no choice but to sell the business. I came back to Melbourne—Terry went to America—and I ended up working for my ex-partner from Shakahari. And I decided to go back to university on my own terms. I studied history.

And six months later, Terry came back. When he came back, he didn't want me to work in a restaurant. He didn't want me to finish university. But I would go to university, go to work at the restaurant, and come back at eleven o'clock when he was asleep. I would cook him dinner on Saturday and Sunday for the five nights of the week. They were all labeled: MONDAY, TUESDAY, WEDNESDAY . . . That's what you do for love, right? You bend over backward for the other person. That's what I did, because I was so in love.

Then television found me. That was quite funny. They needed somebody who could understand food and be able to communicate. I was called in for an audition and I thought, *It must be a hoax or a fake call.* I can still remember walking to Terry's little home office and saying, "Guess what happened? I've just been asked to go for a TV interview." And he said, "Nah." And I said, "Yes, that's what I think, too: *Nah.*"

It was called *Food Lovers' Guide to Australia.* It was an eighteen-part series. It was enormously successful. That took me back into national attention again. For me, it was a lark and just fun. I can still remember asking Terry, "Me? The little boy from a tiny fishing town in Malaysia, going on national television?"

*After the show, Tony started a cooking school, which he called the Tony Tan Cooking School. He was educating eager students not only about cooking techniques, but about history as well. There were hands-on classes and demonstration classes. This was, he realized, his calling.*

It was wonderful. We had all kinds of foods: modern Australian, modern Chinese. We had chefs like Ben Shewry from Attica coming to cook for us. It was fun; I loved it. I realized a lot of people in the public sphere don't really know quite as much as we do, which was a surprise to me. You give as much information as possible, and then you build on that history, you build on that culture. Not only would people learn about a dish, they would also take home the background behind it. I think this is really relevant, because there are misconceptions as to what Asian food is all about, particularly when you are living in a Caucasian or Western culture. Asian food, except for Japanese food, is really much misunderstood. There is still a wall, but we keep breaking it down.

Two thousand nine was the year that Terry walked out on me. I was absolutely distraught. When Terry and I split, I couldn't even run the cooking school. I was that bad. When the relationship ended, [Terry and his lawyer] literally took everything. They took away my cooking school, my livelihood.

*In the years since his cooking school closed, Tony has stayed active in the Melbourne food scene. He gives food tours in Australia and Asia; he continues to be a presence at food festivals and beyond. He's*

My parents always had chickens. They grew their own vegetables. I want that. I really, really want that. I want to go out there and pick my own peas. I want to go out there and pick my own broccoli. I want to go out there and say, "Okay, these are my own watercress." I love watercress, especially in Chinese-style soups.

Our lives turn out very differently from the lives that were expected of us—all because we moved somewhere else. Sometimes I try to imagine what my life would have been like if my family had stayed in Malaysia, if I hadn't met this or that person—how my fate might have turned out differently.

It's pretty amazing to think about what our parents really expect of us and how we turn out to be something else. Maybe it was written in the stars, or maybe it's our own personalities, our road of discovery.

My parents built an incredible bond with each other that came from a long process of understanding. They were almost inseparable. When my father died, his last breath was calling my mother's name. He used to hold her hand in public. I can remember they would sit outside in the breeze and feel the evening air.

*Do you feel like you want that? "Of course. Wouldn't you?" Tony says. Playing that game of "what if," I wonder if our dreams themselves would have been different if life hadn't taken our families, Tony's and mine, away from Malaysia—if we would have been happier with something else, or less.*

In some ways, I tend to think that we're very lucky in the sense that we were born in Malaysia, but we are no longer pure, we've been appropriated somewhat. Despite the problems that we face as Asians, we are able to weave our way through life far better than people in Asia or any people who come from a monoculture.

It's only in the past ten or fifteen years that I've begun to be more and more aware of my own being, and I like that. Suddenly I'm aware that I have a voice, suddenly I'm aware that I have made a contribution to society.

As a cook, I've created an awareness. As an Asian Australian, I think I've helped to bridge the gap between Asian Australians and Caucasian Australians. I think that I'm one of those very lucky Asians here who are able to cross over.

I love teaching and I love communicating. I've been given a voice. To know that I've actually contributed something to this society or culture, it's actually quite a nice feeling.

Every once in a while, you take two steps forward and one step back. But what can you do? Either you give up, or you keep fighting. This is how I feel: I've got to keep fighting.

# The Good Stuff Doesn't Sit Still

Cemre Narin

*Siyez* is the mother of all wheat, the oldest variety still in existence. Humans first began cultivating it ten thousand years ago, because its husks can endure cold winters, where other varieties fail. It is high in protein and low in gluten—an ancient superfood.

We are standing in the middle of a field of *siyez* right before harvest in July. The head-high stalks stretch out like a giant yellow-green carpet, waving gently as far as the eye can see. This is Kastamonu, a charming Turkish province in the foothills of Mount Ilgaz, near the Black Sea, where nearly seven hundred farmers grow the ancient crop. Most of them dry and crack the husked grains to make bulgur, to be used in fragrant pilafs.

*Siyez* bulgur is not nearly as common as bulgur made from durum wheat, but it's become a sought-after product in some big city markets and restaurants. This is a fairly new development. Until about fifteen years ago, most of us in Turkey had not even heard of *siyez*. Even here in Kastamonu, its homeland, *siyez* was basically considered cattle feed.

Almost invisible amid the branches of wheat are three men who can be credited for *siyez*'s recent star turn. One is Mustafa Afacan, the owner of the field and a farmer who dedicates his life to raising *siyez* to prominence. An active journalist as well, his piercing eyes stand out from a shroud of long black hair and an equally impressive beard. He looks as resolute as a Hittite king.

Tangör Tan, full-time researcher of Anatolian foodways

Then there is Mehmet Gürs, the visionary chef of the restaurant Mikla. Since his arrival in Istanbul in the nineties, the half–Finnish-Swedish, half–Turkish forty-seven-year-old has been a provocative figure in the country's culinary world. Perhaps most notably, he is responsible for starting a movement he has dubbed the "New Anatolian Kitchen."

Anatolia, also called Asia Minor, is the peninsula of land bounded to the north by the Black Sea, to the east and south by the Mediterranean Sea, and to the west by the Aegean Sea. Today it mainly constitutes the Asian part of Turkey. A crossroads throughout history, it is both geographically and culturally the bridge between East and West. The idea behind the New Anatolian Kitchen is to preserve traditional food sources from the region, while helping them evolve through their use in creative kitchens. Since its inception eight years ago, the movement has shone a light on hundreds of largely forgotten ingredients like *siyez* and on growers like Afacan. Following Gürs's lead, more and more modern chefs and cooks in big cities have embraced Anatolian produce and traditions.

At Mikla, Gürs cooks *siyez* bulgur with spices, and turns it into ice cream to be served alongside confit apricots from the Eastern Anatolian town of Malatya. It is nutty, fragrant, and completely original, but at the same time reminiscent of *aşure*, a classic porridge-like dessert usually made with barley and cracked wheat.

Standing beside Gürs and Afacan is Mikla's full-time researcher on the road, Tangör Tan. He's wearing a large colorful scarf around his neck and a big smile on his face. Tan is the link between chef and farmer—the man who travels all around Anatolia exclusively on Mikla's behalf, seeking out exceptional products and chasing almost-forgotten traditions. For the past eight years, Tan has been traveling throughout Turkey and its neighboring countries in his cozy silver Renault. He drives 65,000 kilometers a year and spends about two hundred fifty days on the move, visiting tiny Anatolian villages. The forty-two-year-old researcher has amassed a superb knowledge of Anatolian products and culture. He is the guy you want to be with on an expedition for *Kars kaşar* cheese by the eastern border, foraging for wild plants on a hilltop in the Aegean, or looking for the most aromatic pepper flakes at the local market.

It is quite a luxury for a restaurant in Turkey—or anywhere in the world, for that matter—to have someone in a full-time position like this. But in a country as intricate and diverse as this one, the only way to keep up is to have someone like Tan in the field.

Turkey is not a large country, but its biodiversity is on par with that of a small continent. It is encircled by three seas, with coasts, forests, mountains, rivers, wetlands, and a spectacular richness of resources. Anatolia features Siberian, Persian, and Mediterranean ecosystems. It has more than ten thousand plant species, around one-third of which are endemic. It is home to fallow deer and pheasant. One of the region's three major migratory bird routes passes through here. It's a biodiversity superpower, as well as a cultural, religious, and ethnic crossroads.

But the reality is that this diversity is under threat. Between the needs of an eighty-million-strong population, heavy migration away from rural areas, industrial farming, and insufficient governmental conservation efforts, products and foodways are disappearing at a rapid clip. It is becoming increasingly difficult to find *lüfer*, the feisty Bosphorus blue fish; or *taşköprü sarımsağı*, the aromatic garlic from Kastamonu; or farmers who use sound methods, favor heirloom varieties, and care about preserving their environment and their culture. It's a common story around the globe.

The underlying mission of the New Anatolian Kitchen—and Tan's relentless wanderings—is to help protect the legacy of the region by building a new culinary vision that can sustain Anatolian producers, without regard for ethnic, national, or religious boundaries.

*Tarhana*, a fermented
and dried mixture of
cereals, vegetables,
and yogurt used as a
base for soups

Tan was born and raised in Nazilli, a small, sunny town in the Aegean surrounded by mountains. He has a relaxed and happy nature. His charming accent, which becomes thicker when he speaks with villagers and local producers, is one that immediately puts other people at ease. His eyes are soft but inquisitive—they give away his intelligence and knowledge immediately.

After finishing high school in Izmir, the nearest big city to Nazilli, Tan went on to university to study agricultural engineering "for no particular reason," he says, as we talk on our six-hour drive back to Istanbul from Kastamonu. He continues, "My first choice was to become a veterinarian. I love animals! I couldn't get in, so I got stuck with my second choice, which was agricultural engineering." He liked it nevertheless and made the most of his studies, which even took him to the Scottish Rural University College, where he worked as a research assistant in the Highlands. During and upon graduation from university, he worked in restaurant kitchens to make money. His plan was to continue with school to earn his master's degree and eventually become an academic.

Things took an unexpected turn when a renowned chef from Istanbul offered Tan a job at her restaurant. A couple of restaurant jobs

*Maraş tarhanası* is a chip-like variety of *tarhana*, often eaten as a snack.

later, he found himself working at Numnum, a casual dining establishment owned by Gürs. "I would make cheesecake and Caesar salad," Tangör reminisces. "And in my spare time, I would read all the books that Mehmet kept on the shelves." This curiosity and appetite for learning caught Gürs's attention. He encouraged Tan to apply to the Slow Food organization's University of Gastronomic Sciences in Italy.

Tan received a full scholarship and spent three and a half years in Italy, studying under Slow Food's founder, Carlo Petrini. He studied gastronomy, but benefited most from his internships in the field. He learned about cheese, beer, wine, bread, fish, and the processes that brought these foods to the table. He went to Ireland to work in breweries, to South Australia to study wine, and to Australia's Kangaroo Island to learn about cheese making.

Upon Tan's return from Italy in 2009, Gürs hired him, gave him a car, and sent him on the road. "What made me hire him was his great palate," says Gürs. "Tangör really knows great from good. He also has an easygoing attitude and, most important, great people skills. When on the road, in a new environment, you have to be very, very adaptable. To really get on the inside, you have to be patient and really honest with the people you meet. You end up as family. That is when a true relationship starts."

One more variety of *tarhana*, made with red pepper and kaymak cheese

At first, Tan didn't know where to look. He started with his hometown of Nazilli and traveled around the sunny coastal Aegean region. He took tips from trusted sources and followed one lead to another, until eventually, he stumbled into some interesting producers.

One was an eighth-generation *helva* maker named Tıflıpaşa, from Edremit, about a six-hour drive from Istanbul. The family had been in the *helva* business since the 1700s, but its hand-churned *helva* and tahini were little known in Istanbul. Tan took a sample of their golden, twice-roasted tahini back to Mikla, where Gürs and the kitchen team were impressed with its flavor as well as its heritage and decided to use it right away. "Our initial thought was to make *helva* ice cream, but then we decided we couldn't mess with such a perfect product," Mehmet recalls. They decided to serve the tahini drizzled over candied pumpkin.

Today, Mikla works with a network of about three hundred small producers in Anatolia. An elderly couple in the Aegean sells them *kopanisti*, a pungent cheese made from the milk of *kara keçi*, a local goat breed. Gürsel Tonbul, a farmer near the coastal town of Kuşadası who employs and supports village women in the region, supplies the restaurant with organic fruit vinegars, more specifically, a super-concentrated fig vinegar. Aşkın and Şiraz Demir, an Orthodox

Christian couple from a small village in Antakya, 12 kilometers away from the Syrian border, are the producers of tiny green olives called *halhalı*. Mikla serves them as snacks alongside white chickpeas.

In Devrek, up in the north, there's a women's cooperative that produces *tarhana*, an ingenious fermented soup base. It's made by mixing yogurt, wheat flour, tomatoes, onion, spices, various vegetables, and the flowering *tarhana* herb, then leaving the thick paste to ferment for several days, during which time it develops an intense, umami-rich flavor. It is then divided up, dried, and crumbled to make *tarhana* powder, which is used as an "instant" soup mix. The co-op ferments its *tarhana* indoors, using exquisite local tomatoes and a special spice mix called *boy*, which includes dried herbs like tarragon, thyme, rosemary, and mint. At Mikla, their *tarhana* is served unconventionally as a thick sauce with grilled octopus, braised leeks, and camel sausage (*deve sucuğu*).

Sometimes it can take years of nurturing a relationship before both sides feel comfortable enough to trust each other to do right by the products. The key to everything is movement. Tan is constantly on the road, largely in order to maintain a connection with all of Mikla's producers at all times. The last time Tan computed the facts of his travels, he figured he'd drunk 11,680 cups of tea, tasted more than 5,000 products, and delivered 312 pieces of Kinder Surprise chocolate to kids in various villages.

He is often received like a family member when he travels. He stays in farmers' homes, drives hundreds of kilometers to attend family celebrations, visits when he learns a producer is sick, and calls just to check in. The majority of the producers Mikla works with are women, so Tan sometimes travels with his wife, Güher Tan. Her presence tends to put people at ease and helps women producers open up.

"It is me being an engineer and working for a reputable restaurant like Mikla that lets me through the door," Tan says. "When they find out I'm an engineer, they ask me questions on how to improve their products. If I don't know the answer, I find out from another farmer and take that information to the one with the problem." This was the case with Keziban and Hüseyin Genç, a couple producing exquisite organic apple vinegars in a small village in Çankırı, for whom Tan located locally crafted oak barrels. Tan often finds himself raveled up in the production of the ingredients he's looking for,

*Erişte* is a hand-cut egg noodle from Anatolia.

doing things like ferrying local chickpeas from a farmer in Kuşadası to another in Karaman, 700 kilometers away.

With time, Tan learns about the products and practices of the people he encounters—where the farmers are originally from, what seeds they use and how they grow them, how they like to prepare their product and whether it's tied to a special occasion, and whether the next generation plans on continuing the parents' work.

Often the bounty from Tan's travels will inspire the kitchen at Mikla, where the menu changes constantly, but it's also up to the kitchen team to give him direction. This may be Gürs, who came across a new salt producer last week and would like Tan to follow up. Or it could be Adem Boğatepe, Mikla's head chef, who recently asked Tan for *yarpuz* (or pennyroyal)—wild mint that grows in the mountains of Kars in northeastern Anatolia.

Cihan Çetinkaya, the corporate chef of Gürs's restaurants, has been working shoulder to shoulder with Tan for years. He says that a recent lead was based on his own childhood. He remembers a molasses called *zile pekmezi* from when he lived in Gerede, in the Bolu Province of the Western Black Sea region. "My grandmother would buy it for me and I would eat it like Nutella," Çetinkaya says. The thick molasses is made from local Narince grapes and egg whites.

It is labor-intensive to produce by hand and has been somewhat forgotten today.

Tan hit the road in pursuit of Çetinkaya's childhood delicacy, and located producers around Anatolia, particularly in the Black Sea region. He spoke with them extensively to find out who was truly making *zile pekmezi* by hand and what kind of grapes, sugar, and eggs they used. He brought samples back to the kitchen for the team to taste. In the end, they settled on a product from Bolu, one that was more intense in flavor and thicker than the other samples. It is currently on the menu in a refreshing dessert with buffalo yogurt, strawberry sorbet, and walnuts.

Anatolia is a complex place. As children growing up here, we're taught about its strategic position between the Middle East, Europe, and Central Asia. In history class, we go back to Neolithic times and learn about the Hittites, the Persians, the Romans, the Seljuks, and the Ottomans who ruled here for thousands of years. Anatolia is the hub through which civilization, religion, and commerce between East and West spread. It's always been at the heart of movement, and it's seen a lot of action. It remains a gateway today: recently, more than three million Syrian refugees passed into Turkey.

The result is that a *meyhane*—a traditional restaurant best described as a Turkish version of a tavern—in Istanbul may feature small plates of *arnavut ciğeri*, Albanian-style liver and onions brought by refugees fleeing the Balkan Wars; hummus from the Arabs in Southeast Turkey; *tarama*, a creamy paste made with fish roe, from the Greeks; and *topik*, a popular Armenian meze made with caramelized onions, currants, pine nuts, and spices mashed together with chickpeas.

While this variety is wonderful, it also makes it difficult to draw a single definition of Anatolian cuisine. Take *keşkek* as an example. The slowly beaten wheat-and-meat dish typical of wedding ceremonies is topped with a butter-and-red-pepper sauce in Tire, but you wouldn't be caught dead serving it like that in Ödemiş, the next town over. "They would literally ostracize you," Tan says, half jokingly.

Gürs specifically writes in his New Anatolian Kitchen manifesto that the movement is about a region rather than nationality or ethnicity. He does not really care for physical or mental borders established by religion, nationality, or ethnicity. It makes sense. Products and food cultures persist despite changes in borders, movement, or the exchange of power between ethnic or religious groups. It's much more about the land itself and the living things on it.

Mikla has been recording and building a database for all the products they have tried—close to seven hundred have been logged already. The information will eventually be made available to the public on a free website. Readers will be able to look up how products are grown and how they taste, which regions they come from, and the local dishes they're used in. They'll learn about products like *divle* obruk, a naturally made cheese stored in a 45-meter-deep cave in Central Anatolia; *lakerda*, pickled fatty bonito; *hardaliye*, a beverage of grape juice with mustard seeds and sour cherry leaves from Trakya; the Tıflıpaşa *helva* made by the family in Edremit; sugar-beet molasses; mud cheese; and Mustafa Afacan's *siyez*.

What started as a selfish search for the best possible products for Mikla has turned into a movement. "When you live and work in an area with so much to offer, it is only natural to want to dig deep and share," says Gürs. He believes that for a product and food culture to survive, it's not enough to try to hold on to it—you have to keep it moving. "Culture is a constantly evolving thing," he says. "The past, present, and future all go hand in hand. It's definitely not about national pride. I would probably have done the same thing if I lived in Australia, South America, or Japan."

A few weeks after we return from Kastamonu, Gürs receives a text message from Mustafa Afacan. It's a clip from the local newspaper: half a page about that day on the *siyez* field, with a photo that Gürs had shared on Instagram.

"It's important that *siyez* and Mustafa Afacan get the attention they deserve," says Gürs. "But it's equally important to me that the next farmer or neighbor sees this and starts growing *siyez*."

Meanwhile, Tan is already back on the road, this time checking up on a black-mulberry farmer in the small Aegean village of Cambazlı. He will see if the recent hailstorm did any damage to the mulberries, and will stay a few days in the farmer's home so he can attend his grandson's high school graduation.

# People Will Eat Anything

Aralyn Beaumont and Marissa Gery

We eat aardvark, multiple species of abalone, achatina snails, acorn barnacles, acrobat ant, Aesop shrimp, African armyworm, African collared-dove, African maize stalk borer, African migratory locust, African mole cricket, African moon moth, African palm weevil, African silkworm, African thief ant, African wild dog, Afro-Asian bollworm, agave snout weevil, akiami paste shrimp, alkali fly, alpaca, Amami woodcock, Amazonian manatee, American anglerfish, American bison (buffalo), American bollworm, American coot, American crocodile, American plaice, American shad, American woodcock, Andean (or spectacled) bear, annual cicada, Antarctic minke whale, Apache cicada, aphid, Arabian camel (and Bactrian camel, too), arapaima, Arctic char, Argentine anchoita, Argentine hake, Argentine sea bass, Argentine shortfin squid, Arrau turtle, arrowtooth flounder, Asian hornet, Asian longhorn beetle, Asiatic black bear, Asiatic rice borer, Atlantic bay scallop, Atlantic bluefin tuna, Atlantic halibut, Atlantic jackknife clam, Atlantic puffin, Atlantic rock crab (peekytoe crab), Atlantic salmon, Atlantic surf clam, Atlantic wolffish, axis deer (chital), auks (great, little, and razor-billed), Australian plague locust, babul-root boring longicorn, backswimmer, bag-shelter moth, Baikal seal, Baird's beaked whale, bamboo borer, bamboo weevil, banana skipper, banded sugar ant, band-tailed pigeon, various species of barracuda, barramundi, basa fish, dozens of bat species, Bawean deer, two species of bearded pig, bearded seal, bearded weevil, Benguela hake, beni-zuwai crab, Bering wolffish, Bess beetle, bigeye tuna, bighead carp, bighorn sheep, black armyworm, black-bellied angler, black caiman, black carp, black cutworm, blackfin goosefish, black fly, black iguana, black palm weevil, black pomfret, black scabbardfish, black sea bass, black sea devil anglerfish, black spotted grasshopper, blackspotted smooth-hound, black swallowtail, black-tailed jackrabbit, blacktip tope, black weaver ant, Blainville's beaked whale, blood clams (also known as blood cockles), blowflies, blue catfish, blue crab, blue grenadier, blue mussel, bluespotted seabream, blue swimmer crab, blue tilapia, blue velvet shrimp, blue whale—along with a couple dozen more whales, which we'll stop listing now, because you get the picture—bobcat, bogong moth, bogue, bollworm, Bombay locust, bonobo, botfly, boto (Amazon River dolphin), broad-snouted caiman, broad-tipped conehead, brown bear, brown huntsman spider, brown locust, brown sandfish, brown smooth-hound, Bukidnon woodcock, bullet tuna, Burgundy snail, Burmeister's porpoise, bushpig, cactus weevil, caddis fly, Calamian deer, California anchovy, California salmonfly, California sea lion, California spot prawn, Cape bushbuck, Cape fur seal, capybara, carabao, carpenter bee, cat, Central American red brocket, Chaco tortoise, chamois, channel catfish, cheetah, chicken (all seventy-plus breeds of them), Chilean nylon shrimp, chinchilla, Chinese mantis, Chinese mitten crab (better known as the highly prized "hairy crab" of Shanghai), Chinese mud shrimp, Chinese tussah silkmoth, Chinese wax scale, Chinese white shrimp, Chinook salmon, chocolate demon butterfly, Christmas beetle, chukar partridge, chum salmon, clear-winged grasshopper, click beetle, clown grasshopper, cochineal insect, cockles of numerous varieties, cockroach, coconut rhinoceros beetle, many fish that fall under the cod umbrella whether they're really cod or not (including black, blue, East Siberian, Eastern freshwater, Eucla, Greenland, ling, Maori, Mary River, Murray, Pacific, pelagic, polar, poor, potato, rock, saffron, sleepy, small-headed, soft, tadpole, and trout—as in the endangered trout cod, not regular trout, which we also eat), coffee locust, coffee berry borer, coho salmon, common bagworm, common carp, common chimpanzee, common cuttlefish, common dab, common grounddove, common emperor moth, common fruit fly, common ling, common octopus, common periwinkle, common shrimp, common wallaroo, over sixty varieties of conch, confused flour beetle, convolvulus hawk-moth, cougar, coyote, coypu, crane fly, crawling water beetles, crowned bullfrog, crucian carp, Cuban crocodile, Cuvier's dwarf caiman, cynthia moth, Dall's porpoise, damselfly, De Witte's clawed frog, death's-head hawk-moth, death's head cockroach, death-watch beetle, deep-water Cape hake, deep-water rose shrimp, desert locust, digger bee, diving beetle, dobsonfly, dog, something like twenty different dolphins, donkey, dorado (also known as mahimahi), dormouse, dory, Dover sole, Dow's puffin, dragonfly, driver ant, drywood termite, 130-plus species of duck and geese, dugong, duiker, dung beetle, Dungeness crab, dusky grouse, earwig, eastern dobsonfly, eastern oyster, Eastern Pacific bonito, Eastern toe-biter (a type of beetle, if you're wondering), edible crab (brown crab), eggfruit and shoot borer, eland, elephant, elephant hawk moth, emperor moth, emu, eri silk-moth, escolar, Eurasian collared-dove, Eurasian coot, Eurasian woodcock, European anchovy, European bass, European cattle, European eel, European flat oyster, European flounder, European hake, European house cricket, European mantis, European plaice, European roe deer, evening cicada, fallow deer, Felidae (cats in general, both wild and domestic), flatheaded appletree borer, flesh fly, flower beetle, freshwater bream, forest francolin, Fraser's clawed frog, Galápagos tortoise, garden snail (and other members of genus *Helix*, some of which have already been mentioned), gazami crab, gerenuk, ghost moth, giant acacia click beetle, giant Asian mantis, giant bamboo weevil, giant California sea cucumber, giant cricket (weta), giant forest ant, giant honey bee, giant metallic ceiba borer beetle, giant prickly stick insect, giant skippers, giant water bug, giant weevil, giant western crane fly, goat, gilthead seabream, gold-dust weevil, golden silk orb-weaver, golden threadfin bream, Goliath birdeater spider, intertidal and pelagic goose barnacles, gorilla, grass carp, grasshopper, gray brocket, gray partridge, gray seal, greater banded hornet, greater sage-grouse, green bush locust, green iguana, green ormer, green tree ant, green valley grasshopper, grooved Tanner crab, grouper, grub, guinea pig, guinea fowl, Gulf flounder, Gunnison sage-grouse, haddock, hairy emperor moth, handsome francolin, harbor porpoise, harbor seal, hard clam, thirty species of hare, harlequin beetle, harlequin cockroach, harp seal, harvester termite, hawkmoth, a great variety of herring, hog deer, honey ant, honeybee, hooded seal, horned puffin, hornet, horse, huaytampu butterfly, huhu beetle, hummingbird hawk-moth, hybrid striped bass, impala, Inca dove, at least three kinds of Indian carp, Indian honeybee, Indian lac insect, Indian tussah silk-worm, Indo-Pacific finless porpoise, Indo-Pacific swamp crab,

Jameson's cream spot, Japanese amberjack, Japanese anchovy, Japanese carpenter bee, Japanese eel, Japanese flying squid, Japanese giant hornet, Japanese oak silkworm, Japanese rhinoceros beetle, Japanese sea cucumber, Japanese wobbegong, Javan woodcock, Jerusalem cricket, jewel beetle, joined-fins skate, Jonah crab, jumbo flying squid, jungle cockroach, no fewer than four kinds of kangaroo, katydid, kina urchin, Kivu clawed frog, klipspringer, knifetooth dogfish, Korean yellowjacket, kudu, Kulsi teak borer, lake fly, lake whitefish, large coast locust, large rice grasshopper, leafhopper, lechwe, lesser armyworm, lesser mealworm, lesser migratory grasshopper, litchi stink bug, little honey bee, little red brocket, llama, various kinds of spiny and large-clawed lobsters, long-headed toothpick grasshopper, longhorn beetle, longan stink bug, longfin squid, longtail tuna, lumpfish, lynx, seventeen species of mackerel, Madagascar lemur, Madagascar locust, Magdalena River turtle, maguey worm, mahogany clams, mallard, mango-tree longicorn borer, manuka beetle, marbled lungfish, marlin, Masai giraffe, mayfly, mealworm beetle, mealy plum aphid, melon bug, mesquite girdler, Mexican fruit fly, mice, migratory locust, mole cricket, various species of monkey, monkeypod roundheaded borer, many species of monkfish (also known as goosefish, allmouth, molligut, and fishing-frog), moose, mopane worm, Morelet's crocodile, Mormon cricket, mountain gorilla, mountain hare, mountain lion, mourning cloak butterfly, mourning dove, Mozambique tilapia, Msasa moth, mud carp, muga silkmoth, mulberry longhorn beetle, mule, mule deer, musk ox, narrow-ridged finless porpoise, New Guinea woodcock, New Zealand green-lipped mussel, night wasp, Nile crocodile, Nile perch, Nile tilapia, North American black bear, North American elk (which is the same thing as red deer and wapiti), North Pacific hake, northern brown shrimp, northern fur seal, northern giraffe, northern june beetle, northern masked chafer, northern prawn, northern pudu, northern red snapper, northern shortfin squid, nursehound, nyala, ocean perch, offshore hake, olive flounder, opah (also known as moonfish), two dozen opossum species, orange roughy, oriental house fly, oriental latrine fly, Orinoco crocodile, oryx, ostrich, Pacific bonito, Pacific geoduck, Pacific halibut, Pacific oyster, Pacific sand lance, paddy bug, pallid emperor moth, palmetto weevil, palm seed bruchid beetle, pampas deer, Panama hake, panda bear, pandora moth, six pangolin species, Patagonian skate, Patagonian squid, pelagic thresher, periodic cicada, permit, Peruvian anchoveta, phantom midge, domestic pig, pigeon, piked dogfish, pine sawyer beetle, pine shoot beetle, pine tree emperor moth, pink bollworm, pink salmon, nearly two dozen piranha species, Pismo clam, thirty-six species of plover, polar bear, pollock, pompano, porbeagle, nearly two dozen species of porcupine, Portuguese dogfish, potter wasp, greater and lesser prairie chickens, predaceous diving beetles, prickly redfish, pine processionary caterpillar, puriri moth, purple sea urchin, pygmy hippopotamus, pygmy hog, quail, queen crab, rabbit (of the desert marsh and swamp varieties, plus a number of domesticated species), raccoon, more than a hundred species of rail, rainbow sardine (in addition to seven other sardine species), rainbow smelt, rainbow trout, over fifty species of rat (including the bandicoot rat, cane rat, wood rat, and so on), nearly thirty species of rattlesnake (and hundreds of other edible snake species), various species of razor clam, redbanded seabream, redbreast tilapia, red brocket, red bug, red deer, red-faced spider monkey, red flour beetle, red-footed tortoise, redheaded Amazon River turtle, red king crab, red-legged grasshopper, red locust, red-necked spurfowl, red palm weevil, red sea urchin, red-spotted shrimp, red stripe weevil, red swamp crawfish (Louisiana crawfish), red tequila worm, reindeer or caribou, reindeer warble fly, reticulated giraffe, rhinoceros, ribbon seal, rice weevil, ringed seal, ring-necked pheasant, roan antelope, rock pigeon, rock ptarmigan, rock shrimp, Rocky Mountain locust, roughskin skate, royal red shrimp, ruffed grouse, sable antelope, sack-bearer moth, Sahelian tree locust, sal heartwood borer, salt marsh moth, sand cricket, sandfish, Savanna side-necked turtle, scaly francolin, scarab beetles, Schneider's dwarf caiman, scup, sea otter, seed beetles, Senegalese hake, shallow-water hake, a few dozen kinds of shark, shark catfish, sharp-tailed grouse, sheep, shore fly, shortspine African angler, Siberian roe deer, sika deer, silkworm, silkworm moth, silver barb, silver carp, silver cyprinid, silver hake, six-tubercled Amazon River turtle, skate, skimmers, skipjack tuna, skippers, slate pencil urchin, slender-snouted crocodile, slug caterpillar, smalleye smooth-hound, smallmouth velvet dogfish, small yellow croaker, twenty species of snipe, snipe fly, snow crab, soft-shell clam, soldier fly, sooty grouse, South American fur seal, South American palm weevil, South American sea lion, Southern African anchovy, southern bluefin tuna, southern flounder, southern giraffe, southern hake, southern pink shrimp, southern pudu, southern brown shrimp, southern rough shrimp, southern white shrimp, southern yellow-jacket, soybean pod borer, spanner crab, spectacled caiman, spider, spiny sea cucumber, spittlebug, spotted camel cricket, spotted grasshopper, spotted pine sawyer, spotted seal, spotted wobbegong, spotted wolffish, springbok, spruce grouse, more than a hundred species of squirrel (plus chipmunks and marmots), stag beetle, steenbok, Steller sea lion, stick insect, stingless bee, stink bug, stink toe, striped catfish, multiple kinds of sturgeon (and their expensive roe), subterranean termite, Sudan millet bug, Sudanese tree locust, Sulawesi woodcock, summer flounder or fluke, sun bear, sundowner moth, superworm, surf clam, swordfish, tahr, tanner crab, tarpon, teak defoliator moth, ten-lined june beetle, Thai zebra tarantula, thorn bug, threadfin, threespot tilapia, thresher shark, tiger beetle, tiger blowfish, tilefish, tip wilter, tobacco hornworm, tomato hornworm, treehopper, trumpeter swan, tsessebe, tucuxi dolphin, tufted deer, tufted puffin, turbot, turkey, twin line lappet moth, twinpoes diving beetle, two-spotted cricket, two-striped grasshopper, two-tailed swallowtail butterfly, Uganda clawed frog, valley grasshopper, velvet belly lantern shark, vulture bee, wahoo, walking catfish, wallaby, walleye, walrus, warble fly, six species of warty pig, water beetle, water boatman, water buffalo, waterbuck, water scavenger beetle, water scorpion, water stick-insect, water strider, Wellington flying squid, West African manatee, western ash borer, western white shrimp, West Indian manatee, white-bellied spider monkey, white-crowned pigeon, whiteleg shrimp, white-lined sphinx moth, white maguey worm, white river crawfish, white-sided jackrabbit, whitespotted sawyer, white-tailed deer, white-tailed ptarmigan, white teatfish, white-tipped dove, white-winged dove, whiting, wild boar, wildcat, wildebeest, willow ptarmigan, willow tree emperor moth, winter flounder, witchetty grub, wolf eel, yak, yam beetle, Yangtze sturgeon, yellowfin tuna, yellow-footed tortoise, yellow goosefish, yellow mealworm, yellownose skate, yellow perch, yellow-spotted river turtle, Yucatán brown brocket, zebra, and zebu, among many other species of insect and animal.

# Culinary Difference Makes a Difference

## Krishnendu Ray

I was in high school when I ate my first kebab—a watershed moment for me that coincided with the first time I used a fork. I had recently moved to Delhi, India, from the small town of Jamshedpur, and needed training in big-city civility. Sartorial acuity, mastering flatware, and developing a stomach for aged cheeses and wine were marks of upward mobility among the class I was delivered into. Consuming kebabs was another kind of cosmopolitan activity, albeit one of a cruder nature, associated with the street rather than the parlor. Kebabs were redolent of a Muslim masculinity that made them irresistible to a Hindu boy such as me.

Meat, especially beef, occupies an excessively marked place in the practices of Hindu vigilantes. When a Hindu crosses over to eating meat, it is a serious threat to caste notions of purity, and thus it is fiercely policed, especially in the current political context. In a recent ruling in which the Indian Supreme Court enunciated the fundamental right to privacy, chief justice Jagdish Singh Khehar wrote: "The right to be let alone is a part of the right to enjoy life. The right to enjoy life is, in its turn, a part of the fundamental right to life of the individual." This newly minted right has energized gay rights activists and critics of Hindu dietary vigilantism. But it will take a lot more work to protect the right to incorporate what you want into your body in places where communitarian demands exceed individual want.

A restaurant in Montego Bay, Jamaica

Contrary to rampant misrepresentation, most Hindus are *not* vegetarian. Most "non-vegs," as the people and the cuisine are often described in India, eat goat meat and fish (rarely any bivalves), in relatively small portions. But kebabs in the Muslim quarter are eyed with particular suspicion among caste Hindus. When I was a kid, my father and uncles, traveling salesmen, used to tell tales of sinful but delectable Muslim food, but it would be years until I had the courage to try my first kebab. My trepidations about eating meat were residues of the long civilizing process regulating Bengali Hindu desires, wherein hot, sour, and meaty are antithetical to domesticated taste. Nationalists repeatedly condemn—in the past and increasingly again—tamarind, chili, and especially unclean meat, associating them with uneducated rural women or casteless men from the uncouth urban bazaar. Yet it is perhaps this very repression that produced an efflorescence in a counterculture of street foods, the lure of *dustu-khide* ("unruly appetite") straining against the claims of decency.

Walking home from school that fateful day, an aroma lured me into the Muslim quarter. Under the shadow of Sufi saint Nizamuddin Auliya's shrine and past Humayun's Tomb, I was drawn into a narrow, winding street, crowded by men in skullcaps. The call of the muezzin from the minarets scattered pigeons from the spires. I was a meek, middle-class Hindu boy adrift in the intimate core of a Muslim neighborhood in the great layered cosmopolis of Delhi. Fanning the flames of a waist-high charcoal grill with a stitched palm frond, the *kebabwala* peddled his wares across the street from the daunting mosque. The aroma of charred flesh was irresistible. I had just enough money for two boti kebabs, which he pulled from the fire with a wad of newspaper and emptied into a stitched-leaf bowl. The kebabs glistened, sputtering heat and juice, wafting accents of clove, cinnamon, and pepper. The smell of charcoal-grilled skewers under the shadow of the *dargah* (shrine) persists as a sensory memory of distancing myself from the enclosures of Brahmanism. Indulging in grilled meat was seen as one in a series of liminal points from boyhood to manhood in my community of middling Hindus. In breaking parental-priestly rules, I was imbibing lessons of multicultural democratic citizenship. Of course, eating kebabs does not *necessarily* lead to open-mindedness, but it was crucial to my personal reeducation. It was entangled with a ressentiment of class, too, of a barely middle-class provincial kid against big-city Hindu superiors. There was something brewing in me, some oppositional relationship to state-parent dietetics that hankered for the unruly kebab. That taste—and the justifications I proffered once my transgression was discovered—was one of the things that stopped me from becoming a Hindu nationalist, I think.

Years later, the smell of burnt meat came to be associated in my mind with the mass murder of Sikh men, many incinerated alive, in the wake of Indira Gandhi's assassination by her Sikh bodyguard. As I roamed the city in despair, I could smell the odor of virulence. Since then, it has become impossible to presume the innocence of something as simple as blistered meat.

I grew up in a context of violence: not just symbolic brutality, but physical, murderous bloodshed between Hindus and Muslims, Hindus and Sikhs, and Odiya and Bengali Hindus. These experiences provided me with two lessons: (1) my palate is more open-minded than my mind, or at least my mind follows my tongue; and (2) a vegetarian ethic and aesthetic can sit quite comfortably alongside violence against others, as we see all around India today in the pitiless lynching of meat-eating Muslims and Dalits.

It makes me wonder: Did I leave India for the United States because I was hungry for flavors less demanding of my loyalty? And if so, did I find them? If not, do such flavors exist anywhere?

## Culinary Misappropriation

In America and other predominantly white countries, a discussion about culinary appropriation has erupted in recent years. Fierce debate has arisen over what it means to eat food originally imagined by one race or ethnicity but cooked by another—such as, say, tacos being prepared by a white chef and sold to predominantly white customers in a fine-dining setting. This debate is important because it engages with the question of power in the making of a culture. Of course, people borrow each other's culinary techniques and dishes all the time, and they should. It would be a terrible world if we were all cloistered within our closed cultural ecumenes. Human history is replete with borrowed edibles, from the chilies of the New World that flavor the otherwise mundane foods of South and Southeast Asia, to indigenous Peruvian potatoes that provide sustenance in Ireland and India, to the enticement of Jewish fish and chips in London or fried artichokes in Rome. But there is an important distinction that must be made about the situation of African Americans.

African Americans have been historically represented in culinary work as slaves, servants, and professionals (in railroads and hotels), yet they get little credit for American culinary culture. In his foreword to *The Jemima Code*, the writer John Egerton counted about a hundred thousand cookbooks produced in more than two centuries of American history, and African Americans get acknowledgment for a measly two hundred, which underrepresents their ratio both as a population and as cooks.

The historian and author Jessica Harris shows us an alternative African American culinary thread that includes chefs such as Hercules (George Washington's cook) and James Hemings (Thomas Jefferson's), and "Big House cooks who prepared lavish banquets, caterers who created a culinary co-operative in Philadelphia in the nineteenth century, a legion of black hoteliers and culinary moguls, and a growing black middle and upper class." In contrast, the standard story of African Americans as merely cheap labor is an exemplary case of misrepresentation of black culinary contribution.

In my own process of becoming an American, I acquired new prejudices. My informal education inevitably included absorbing racist stereotypes about the relationship between fried chicken, chitterlings, watermelon, and blackness. African Americans have been both consigned to eat such foods out of necessity and condemned for doing so. It is one of many examples of how poor people everywhere are censured for being poor and for consuming what they can afford. Eventually I realized there was more to these stereotypes than I had fathomed. The writing of Jessica Harris, Psyche Williams-Forson, Michael Twitty, and Kyla Wazana Tompkins have contributed substantially to my reeducation as a new American. They are incensed when others appropriate or erase the black experience. Williams-Forson calls the homogenization of black taste into fried chicken and black-eyed peas *culinary malpractice*. That is a useful term.

So I think the phrase *cultural misappropriation* should be used in this specific and restrictive case of the experience of African Americans in the United States. In contrast, the American attitude toward Native American culinary culture is not misappropriation but forced assimilation via land colonization, physical displacement, and the imposition of a war-refugee diet of cheap carbohydrates (a pattern that can be found in other settler-colonial cultures, such as Australia, New Zealand, etc.). Yes, there is unaccounted appropriation of cultivars like corn, various squashes, beans, and various kinds of shellfish and meats, but the nature of that relationship is different from the way we are silent on the unacknowledged work of African Americans.

In the case of immigrant culinary cultures in America, which is the primary domain of my expertise and experience, we have what I call culinary subordination, followed by selective upward mobility of white ethnics (Italians, Jews, Spaniards, and Greeks being the important cases) and then Asians (Japanese, Korean, and soon Chinese) partly following the logic of capital accumulation. In short, as a national economy moves up the ladder of development, its culture, including culinary culture, is bestowed with new upper-class connotations, as we have seen happen most dramatically with Italian and Japanese food.

Funneling the concerns of different groups into the umbrella term *cultural appropriation* inadequately represents the history of race, culture, and power dynamics in the trajectory of culinary objects, and it obfuscates the different outcomes awaiting the fate of the labor of different races and ethnicities. Those we classify as being of a different race, for example, have much bigger obstacles to overcome than those we classify as being of different ethnicities.

## Not Foreign but Not the Same

What has retroactively come to be seen as "American cuisine" was first developed by the wave of twenty million or so northern European migrants from England, Scotland, Germany, and Ireland who settled the land by displacing Native Americans. These settler-colonists developed the basic framework for the American palate based on their own tastes; Native American produce such as corn, beans, and squash; and techniques and ingredients brought by enslaved Africans.

From the 1880s to 1924, the American palate underwent a great transformation. The center of demographic gravity shifted during this period to out-migrating peoples from the Mediterranean, including Italians, Greeks, Armenians, and urban minorities from northern Europe such as Polish Jews. It is the food of these groups that Americans first considered markedly "different." This included olive oil, garlic, rosemary, schmaltz, bagels, pizza, olives, pasta, sardines, artichokes, wine, new vegetables such as broccoli, and herbs and spices like anise, coriander, fennel, cumin, and thyme. This is also the time (around the 1910s) that chop suey became a trend, although Chinese immigration to the United States had been greatly curtailed since 1882.

Food in America transforms roughly every forty years, and cuisines once considered "ethnic" become swallowed into the idea of what is American.

American nutritionists, home economists, social reformers, and schoolteachers were endlessly complaining, especially in the Progressive Era, about how terrible all this food was, how terrible the hygiene of its preparation was, and how it provoked—horror of horrors!—the craving for alcohol. They tried to cure Italians and Jews of these terrible food habits. Thankfully, the reformers failed. American food culture is a dynamic, disruptive, agile domain, analogous to the environment surrounding popular music since the 1960s. Almost no other national food culture is as capable of absorbing influences and reshaping itself as American culture. American cuisine changes about every forty years, and that is a good thing because it makes the American palate more interesting. Such a transformation is a sign of the economic and cultural integration of its migrant populations, unlike what is found, for instance, in many European countries. America is in the midst of a third great transformation in taste that began in 1965, with another thirty million immigrants entering from Asia, Latin America, and the Caribbean, adding avocados, cilantro, chilies, mangoes, jicama, curries, *mole*, noodles, tacos, soy, and sushi to the American culinary fabric.

Since the United States began tracking occupations and birthplace, beginning with the 1850 Census, data show a strong correlation between food service occupations and new immigrants. The classifications have changed over time—for instance, cooks, servers, and chefs have been added to the mix of occupations—but we can see that the foreign-born numerically dominate certain occupations, such as domestic servants, hotel and restaurant employees, hotel-keepers, saloon-keepers and bartenders, traders and dealers in groceries, bakers, and butchers. In contrast, members of the so-called white-collar occupations have mostly been native born.

According to the 2000 US Census, 75 percent of restaurant cooks in New York City were foreign born, with the dominant countries and regions of origin being Mexico, Central America, the Caribbean Basin, South America, China, and the former USSR. By 2010, nearly half of all small business owners living in New York City were immigrants, including 69 percent of restaurant owners. Most of the approximately nine thousand street food vendors in New York City today are foreign born, with Bengali as the most common native tongue, followed by Cantonese, Fulani, Arabic, Spanish, Urdu, Wolof, Swahili, etc.

Even as far back as the 1950 Census, after immigration had subsided following restrictions in 1924, 64 percent of restaurant cooks were foreign born (with Italians at the top, followed by Greeks, Chinese, and Germans). By the mid-twentieth century, Italians ran more than ten thousand grocery stores, almost a thousand butcher shops, and more than a thousand restaurants in the city. According to the historian Andrew Smith, Italian American grocers would introduce various kinds of seafood, ice cream, "olive oil, Parmesan cheese, anchovies, pastas, and coffees" to Americans. This was also about the time the word *ethnic* was born in American usage.

In the United States, the term *ethnicity* came into play almost simultaneously across the fields of American journalism and the social sciences in the late 1950s. Back then, it was considered a relatively neutral way of constructing difference without falling into the problems of race. By the late 1980s, ethnicity was seen as a benign claim of cultural coherence by any group below the nation-state level, previously excluded from the centers of power.

An immigrant who enters the American national space, especially a visibly different immigrant, has been turned into an "ethnic" in the last half century. An ethnic is a proximate but subordinate other—too close to be foreign, too different to be the self. According to the twentieth-century sensory regime of Americanism, an ethnic person looks different, sounds different, and prefers different food. Among subcultural and avant-garde groups, the term and the people it describes are sometimes presumed to carry the promise of cultural creativity.

Much of the academic literature about ethnicity and entrepreneurship attends to economics and politics, as if immigrants are creatures only of political economy who never think about taste or beauty or how such things might intersect with the practical-moral universe. The propensity to ignore foreign-born influence in the academic discussion of taste may be a product of the tendency to see discussions of taste as marginal to the real lives of marginal peoples. In this conception, poor, hardworking people can teach us about poverty and suffering, hierarchy and symbolic violence, but never about taste. That might be one of the unfortunate consequences of the overwhelming dominance of the French sociologist Pierre Bourdieu's framework of analysis, which is, at its core, a theory of downward flow of ideas of good taste and exclusively a domain of cultural domination by elites. As a consequence, taste loses its contested and dynamic character.

Although both immigrants and African Americans have a long and substantial presence in US food culture, they have rarely been studied by scholars. As an example, although the Chinese have dominated the feeding occupations from the middle of the nineteenth century, we did not get a book-length treatment of their perspective in establishing and running the quintessential American ethnic restaurant until the twenty-first century in Jennifer 8. Lee's *The Fortune Cookie Chronicles: Adventures in the World of Chinese Food*. That is an extraordinary deferral.

## Recuperating Traveling Tastes

Tastes travel and they travel well, obviously in terms of produce, as seen in the history of potatoes, chilies, spices, and tomatoes, and stimulants such as coffee, tea, and chocolate. Less obviously, tastes have also traveled well via immigrant-designed food businesses in global cities that sell pizza, pasta, lo mein, kebabs, and haute French cuisine, not to mention American Southern cooking brought by African American migrants. Young and professional urban dwellers have been amenable to changing their palates, and in doing so provided new possibilities in the political economy and cultural politics of migrant inhabitation (internationally and intranationally).

Foreigners have always fed Americans, and Americans have eaten it up. That transaction is central to the kinds of democratic openings in American culture that are tough to match almost anywhere else in the world. But the question persists: Does eating other people's food make us more open to engaging with them? It did with me in Delhi and in New York, but for every person like me, there will be a Hindu who reacts with disgust toward a kebab and disdain toward the Muslim vendor selling it. In America, there were many who loved chop suey while hating the Chinese immigrant after the Chinese Exclusion Act, and today many continue to fantasize about soul and Southern food while eliding the contribution of African Americans to that repertoire.

There is no guarantee that eating another's food makes us more tolerant toward him. Yet it can be guaranteed that if I am filled with disgust and disdain toward another's food, there is a greater probability that I will not accommodate him within my framework of civic toleration. We have evidence of that, regarding beef consumption in contemporary India. Caste Hindus are routinely filled with disdain and disgust for the food of lower castes, outcastes, Muslims, and Christians.

Michael Twitty, writing in 2017 in the aftermath of a vitriolic and ultimately violent clash between white supremacists and opposing protesters in Charlottesville, Virginia, said, "I never hated white people for their strange relationship to us, their colored kith and kin, but I grew up with the suspicion that they had no clue just how much of us there was in their family trees and stories and bloodlines and on their groaning tables. Maybe if they did, we would know less enmity toward one another." Refusing to eat another's food out of disgust is symptomatic of xenophobia—it is no surprise that eating (and sleeping together) has been the greatest threat to segregationists by race and by caste across the continents where I have lived.

# There Is No Such Thing as a Nonethnic Restaurant

## Paul Freedman

The words *ethnic* and *restaurant* appear side by side in a 1964 *New York Times* article by Craig Claiborne in which the renowned food critic discusses the culinary offerings in San Francisco. Those two words, *ethnic restaurant*, subsequently became a commonplace phrase used to describe American dining establishments (supposedly) serving East Asian or Latin American food. However, the phenomenon is much older than Claiborne's mention of it.

Americans of varied or no particular ethnic identification have dined at restaurants showcasing the food of immigrants since the late nineteenth century. Today the word *ethnic* as a category of eatery has fallen out of favor because of the implied contrast to some imagined "normal" cuisine. Some might find the word *foreign* more innocuous, but it still assumes that we know what such food is set against: what nonforeign, "normal" food might be.

In the United States, where there is no clear, agreed-upon national cuisine, questions linger. Is American food a collection of mostly forgotten regional specialties such as Southern beaten biscuits and Boston baked beans? Or do a few regional survivors like gumbo and clam chowder—themselves descendants of foreign traditions—constitute a cuisine? Maybe, as many people outside the United States believe, American food is McDonald's and KFC. What I'd like to examine is the peculiar popularity of so-called ethnic food in the

United States and the normative cuisine against which ethnic food seems exotic.

While today most large European cities feature dozens of different imported cuisines, this is a fairly new trend. In 1965, the *Guide Michelin* for Paris listed about 250 restaurants, of which more than 93 percent were French. Eleven were Italian, two were Chinese; there was an Indonesian place, along with two "Oriental or North African" restaurants. This is hardly surprising or scandalous. In 1965, the French preferred French food. Even now, notwithstanding the international spread of pizza, burgers, shawarma, and bubble tea, many European countries (especially in the Mediterranean) still have relatively few foreign restaurants. Sushi is ubiquitous in Barcelona, but this is a twenty-first-century development. Despite its large former colonial empire, Spain has had almost no interest in the food of Latin America, Morocco, or the Philippines. *Arroz a la cubana* is no more Cuban than *ensaladilla rusa* is reminiscent of Russia.

In the United States, by contrast, the popularity of restaurants serving the cuisine of other countries was already well established 130 years ago. An 1893 article in *Frank Leslie's Popular Monthly* boasted that New York offered a unique culinary internationalism where it was possible to "breakfast in London, lunch in Berlin, dine in Paris, and sup in Vienna." While the article acknowledged that Paris might be superior for its mastery of the most prestigious food, New York was unmatched for variety.

Two cuisines in particular have been preeminent: Chinese and Italian.

## Chinese and Italian Restaurants

What came to be known as the Chop Suey Craze began in 1896 when a Chinese envoy (described in the newspapers as a "Viceroy") named Li Hong Zhang visited the United States. Conflicting legends have it that Li Hong Zhang's chef introduced chop suey to America, or alternatively, that it was served for the first time at a reception in the envoy's honor given at New York's Waldorf Hotel. An article in the *New York Journal*, entitled "Queer Dishes Served at the Waldorf by Li Hung Chang's Chicken Cook," defined "chow chop sui" as fricasseed giblets. The giblets part was correct, as *chop suey* is an approximation of the Cantonese term for "entrails." The truth, however, is that chop suey—a jumbled stir-fry of meat, egg, cabbage, and other vegetables, served over rice—was already being offered in Chinatown restaurants across the United States, mostly to non-Chinese patrons. But beginning in 1896, chop suey spread like wildfire, along with its cousin, chow mein, which substitutes fried noodles for rice. By 1903, there were more than a hundred chop suey restaurants in New York City *outside* of Chinatown, especially along Third and Eighth Avenues. Rumors were already rife that the dish was not authentic, but other than a few sophisticates, no one cared about authenticity.

As with Chinese restaurants, the key moment for Italian restaurants was when people who identified as neither immigrant nor "ethnic" started showing up at restaurants in Italian neighborhoods in the 1890s. Italian food arrived in the United States accompanying a large-scale migration from the southern Italian mainland and Sicily. Urban "bohemians" liked the hearty, inexpensive dishes, large portions, and copious amounts of cheap wine, as well as the dining atmosphere, designed to appear spontaneous and carefree. Paralleling the case of chop suey, a repertoire of American adaptations developed, such as spaghetti with meatballs and chicken Parmesan, dishes with only a vague resemblance to what was eaten in Italy.

After the First World War, Italian restaurants departed from the cozy, Chianti-bottle-with-a-candle model of New York's Greenwich Village or San Francisco's North Beach to create a large, flamboyant ambience with strolling musicians and other refinements of what passed for Italian dolce vita, attracting a largely non-Italian audience. The now-closed Mamma Leone's in New York's theater district was founded in 1906 as simply "Leone's," and after a period in which Luisa Leone actually cooked for a small clientele, it became the largest restaurant in the United States, feeding more than *two thousand* people a night from the 1960s to the 1980s. By the 1970s, the restaurant, with its seven-course antipasto, classical statues, and flirtatious waiters, was patronized almost exclusively by out-of-town tourists.

The rise of pizza, originally a preparation common among the poor of Naples, shows the extent to which the United States absorbed and mutated Italian cuisine. American pizza was more about the cheese, tomatoes, and toppings than the dough; and while its popularity grew more slowly than chop suey's, it was ubiquitous after the Second World War. Also unlike chop suey, it has never waned in popularity.

In the case of Chinese and Italian food, therefore, one can see a process by which a nonimmigrant audience becomes familiar with a version of a foreign cuisine adapted to American tastes that then takes on sufficient diffusion and importance within everyday life to become a part of what is meant by "American food." It is impossible to write a history of American dining that ignores either of these cooking traditions. They are still categorized as "ethnic" food, but are a familiar part of our landscape (there are about forty thousand Chinese restaurants in the United States today), and at this point, the dishes we know from Italian American and Chinese American restaurants are more American than Italian or Chinese.

### French and German Cuisine: Normative Prestige and Assimilation

Not all foreign food qualifies as "ethnic." German food has been both assimilated into American food habits while remaining a relatively unsuccessful foreign-restaurant category. French cuisine, for centuries the standard of international fine dining, has never been just another ethnic style of cooking.

German food in America is a peculiar example of a foreign cuisine that is not consistently considered ethnic. Successive waves of Germans immigrated during the colonial and early national periods. After the country's failed revolution of 1848, new arrivals from Germany established influential food businesses, bringing such things as lager beer and egg noodles to the attention of Americans. Germans opened taverns and beer gardens where the food was as important as the drinks, and both were served in a festive, casual, and democratic manner. Observers were struck, on balance favorably, that men brought their wives and children to beer gardens, making them, in effect, the first family restaurants.

To be sure, as with all immigrant groups, the Germans were the object of jokes about the suspicious ingredients going into their food: "How could you be so mean, to grind up all those doggies in your hot dog machine?" as one popular bit of comedic verse had it. This ridicule gained little purchase, however. German food was not only accepted, but certain items became sufficiently popular to be regarded as American, a process so complete that the original ethnic identities of frankfurters, hamburgers, potato salad, headcheese, and doughnuts have been mostly forgotten, something that never happened with chop suey, tacos, or even pizza. The influence of Germany was absorbed invisibly. What German restaurants remain are resolutely German, with German names for dishes on the menu or flamboyant German decor.

French restaurants have defined fine dining in America for most of its existence. The first famous restaurant in the United States was Delmonico's, a French restaurant established in Lower Manhattan in 1831 by two brothers from the Italian part of Switzerland. In 1840, Antoine Alciatore, also not originally French but rather an Italian who had trained in France, opened an eponymous restaurant in New Orleans that is still in business. Antoine's is now thought of as serving typical Creole cuisine, but for more than a century, it called itself a French restaurant *tout court*. In fact, until relatively recently, Antoine's menu conspicuously did not list crawfish or jambalaya.

The modern restaurant was invented in late-eighteenth-century France, and from the time that Delmonico's and Antoine's opened until the 1980s, the most prestigious restaurants in the United States

With the aid of urban bohemians, Italian cuisine has blended seamlessly into American food.

were French. Craig Claiborne, in the first *New York Times* restaurant guide (1964), gave three stars to eight restaurants in New York City, seven of them French. In the revised 1972 edition, the scale went up to four stars. Four out of the seven winners of the guide's top honors were French establishments. In Seymour Britchky's guide four years later, all four four-star restaurants were French.

So what restaurants have traditionally been considered "ethnic"? A 1938 *New Yorker* cover shows drawings of scenes from eight ethnic restaurants: Japanese, Turkish, Scandinavian, Russian, German, Chinese, Jewish, and Italian. On the left side, several dishes are listed in each category; some are reliable clichés (risotto Milanese, borscht, *moo goo gai pan*), but a surprising number are now obscure: *kissel* (Russian berry dessert), Chinese duck *yat garm* (duck with noodles), Turkish eggplant *kizartma*. Missing from the tableau is French cuisine, and this, more than some nebulous concept of "American cuisine," was the definition of normal as opposed to ethnic food, at least at the top end of the prestige ladder.

Even in the nineteenth century, French restaurants were not considered "ethnic"; they represented an international standard to which elite American cuisine tried to adjust itself. And not only in the United States, but all over the world. The menu served in 1910 at the grand Hotel des Indes in Batavia, Dutch East Indies (now Jakarta, Indonesia), reveals no concession to the local cuisine or climate: Consommé Montmorency, Filet de Sole à l'Amiral, Filet de Boeuf Garni à la Chatelaine, Escalopes de Ris de Veau à la Villeroy. On February 22, 1887, King Milan of Serbia dined on *potage à la tortue*, *bouchées à la*

A nominally Italian
meal in America

*reine, saumon à la hollandaise, filets de boeuf à flamande, pâté froid de faisans,
escalopes de chevreuil aux truffes,* and *homard en belle-vue.*

French was an aspirational cuisine. Entrepreneurs in nineteenth-century American boomtowns erected ostentatious restaurants and opera houses to show off wealth and sophistication. In the 1880s, Tombstone, Arizona, had several restaurants whose menus featured mangled French dishes, such as "Croquettes de Voialle aux Aspergus Points" and "Vol au Vent des Huitres, a la Maryland." Even in this untutored locale, French food was expensive, even more so given the trouble of transporting luxury ingredients to the desert.

And therein lies the rub. One reason French food couldn't be considered ethnic was the price. Conventional opinion holds that ethnic restaurants have to be cheap—that is part of their picturesque charm. While the budget ceiling of the ethnic category has been broken in the last thirty years—notably by Japanese and Italian restaurants—this has been accomplished not by renouncing ethnicity, but by defining it in more sophisticated terms, according to subcategories such as regional (Venetian, Roman) or traditional typology (*kaiseki* or *omakase*). These restaurants cease to be ethnic when they become identified as "fine dining." To the extent that Chinese restaurants are still thought of as more ethnic than Italian ones, it is because Italian food has established both low- and high-end representations. Mario Batali's four-star restaurant, Del Posto, isn't considered ethnic, for instance. But before 1990 or so, Italian was seen as just as ethnic as Chinese, if not more so. Both Chinese and Thai food, to take just two examples, have been regionalized as Sichuan and Isaan restaurants, but Americans remain resistant to paying high prices for these cuisines.

The authority of French fine dining was unchallenged in the heyday of Delmonico's—from the 1850s to the 1890s—but it was still the case in the 1950s when Le Pavillon in New York defined haute cuisine and haute status, and even in 1980 when Alice Waters's Chez Panisse in Berkeley was still meticulously French and Lutèce was the best restaurant in New York. The most significant contemporary development in high-end dining in the past several decades has been the eclipse of France as the arbiter of what fine food means. Its decline in the last thirty years has opened up a considerable space for culinary hybridity. In general, these cross-cultural restaurants are too hip and too expensive for diners to lump them together with ethnic restaurants.

## Bohemians and Knowledge of the Exotic

The first members of the American majority to show up at restaurants that had originally been established to cater to homesick immigrants were called, affectionately or derisively, *bohemians*. Here the term *bohemians* refers not to the starving artists of Paris, but to near equivalents of what would later be called "yuppies" and more recently "hipsters"—people with disposable income, living in cities, unmarried, and disdainful of bourgeois aspirations involving children, suburban houses, church, and country clubs. They included journalists, publishers, designers, and others in creative-but-profitable fields, a cohort that was unconventional but not especially rebellious. This group would include white people of Christian backgrounds whose parents were either born in the United States or who emigrated from Britain. Recent immigrants from southern and eastern Europe, as well as Asian and Hispanic Americans, were still "ethnic."

Bohemians sought out picturesque restaurants because they disliked, on the one hand, the stiff formality of elite venues that served French cuisine and, on the other, the gritty atmosphere and poor-quality food of working-men's cafés. The last decades of the nineteenth century saw the rise of middle-class restaurant types that would occupy this intermediate space: luncheonettes, soda fountains, cafeterias, coffee shops, teahouses, and automats catering to office workers, shoppers, and the middle class generally, all of whom tended to be shut out of the extremes of high- and low-end eateries. Ethnic restaurants were part of this middle category, too, but offered appealingly exotic food and quaint ambience.

The bohemians constituted what the technology world now calls "early adopters." Clarence E. Edwords in *Bohemian San Francisco*, a 1914 book that, despite its title, is exclusively about restaurants, recalls the scene before the earthquake of 1906 destroyed the city, when Italian restaurants such as Buon Gusto and Fior d'Italia (the latter still in existence) "appealed to the Bohemian spirit through their good cooking and absence of conventionality, together with the inexpensiveness of the dinners." He laments that Sanguinetti's, once a delightful scene of bohemian festivity, is now patronized by tourists sent there by hotel guides. The narrative of the obscure ethnic restaurant, once known only to the cognoscenti but now spoiled by philistines, remains a persistent trope.

As the mosaic of immigrant groups and their cuisines became a well-established attribute of New York in the twentieth century, new kinds of foreign restaurants were introduced between 1920 and 1970. Like their forebears, they, too, had to negotiate an unstable identity. The sociologist Dr. Krishnendu Ray cites the case of a restaurant called the India Rajah, identified by a guidebook from 1930 as "Turkish (Parsee)" in style. "Upstairs," the guide's author claims, "you will find The Rajah, about as big as a medium-sized clothes press, and not nearly as sanitary; but you're in Turkey now—and if you were terribly fussy, you wouldn't have gone to Turkey in the first place. Besides, the food is worth the trip." It continues:

> The table d'hote starts with Tamarind—a lemon-colored drink made from vegetables—as an appetizer. A watery, albeit true-to-type, native soup follows. Then, the real business of the Turkish dinner sets in. Choose lamb, chicken, or beef curry—oh, such a fiery curry sauce! . . . . You'll enjoy your dinner, speculating about the other queer-looking diners, and learn, astonishingly enough, that all sheiks don't wear goatees, ride white horses and brandish swords.

Eventually the category of Indian restaurant was defined, but this same restaurant, the India Rajah, continued to have trouble with outsiders' understanding of tamarind. Robert Dana, in *Where to Eat in New York* (1948), writes about tamarind extract as "pomegranate nectar . . . a sweet beverage boiled from the tamarind roots that grow on Indian riverbanks."

Indian riverbanks or not, learning that there is such a thing as tamarind shows off a certain degree of knowledge, but yesterday's savoir faire becomes today's comical ignorance. In the 1970s, everyone rejected chop suey for being inauthentic, but General Tso's chicken rode the wave of enthusiasm for Chinese regional cooking. Then it, too, gradually lost prestige to become the butt of jokes.

On the other hand, certain dishes moved from pariah status (i.e., only natives of the foreign country from which they originate can appreciate them) to American staples, the most dramatic example being sushi. As far back as the nineteenth century, the Japanese, aware of Westerners' fondness for meat and aversion to raw fish, created dishes with cooked meat to appeal to Americans in Japan. Newspaper columnists advised American clients of Japanese restaurants in the United States to stick with sukiyaki, teriyaki, or tempura and leave the raw fish for the natives. A 1934 article in the *Los Angeles Times* noted that white Americans often showed up at what the author referred to as "Nipponese" restaurants where sushi was available but "sukiyaki was the favorite." In 1958, a well-known *Los Angeles Times* columnist demurred when presented with the idea that sushi might someday supplant frankfurters, saying, ". . . with the utmost politeness, I'll take a hot dog."

By the 1990s, sushi was not only in the mainstream of American food choices, it was a teen favorite, appealing to what was usually considered a conformist and finicky food demographic. In *The Breakfast Club* (1985), sushi is embraced by the affluent girl but rejected by her less-privileged schoolmates in detention. *Clueless*, a happy satire about high schoolers living in nineties Los Angeles, shows sushi being served at a party without evoking any particular comment. A telling if unheralded moment in the culinary trajectory of *The Sopranos* comes in season six, when, after years of being depicted eating pasta, Tony and Carmela Soprano are shown eating dinner at a sushi restaurant.

## Immigrant Restaurant Owners

Krishnendu Ray's book *The Ethnic Restaurateur* looks at the owners' side of foreign dining. In his treatment of immigrant restaurants, along with other recent books and the documentary *The Search for*

*General Tso*, we can see how food is adapted to American tastes and how chefs navigate the tension between strict interpretation and translation into something familiar. Americans don't like organ meat, so dishes are made with choicer cuts; Americans like sweet ingredients, so "sweet-and-sour" actually becomes just the former.

Some of the women who run Central American food trucks in the Brooklyn neighborhood of Red Hook have added vegetables to Salvadoran *pupusas* because, as one of them told an interviewer, "that's what *blanquitos* expect." For decades, when Red Hook was impoverished and isolated, the women prepared meals on the edges of soccer fields where their friends and relatives were playing. Once an Ikea store was constructed in Red Hook and a ferry from Manhattan started running, the customer base changed and so, therefore, did the food.

Cultural critics debate whether the habit of dining at ethnic restaurants represents a praiseworthy openness to diversity or a sinister form of cultural imperialism. One anodyne extreme of this interpretive spectrum pops up in the *Journal of Popular Culture* in an article by Samantha Barbas entitled "I'll Take Chop Suey." Barbas argues that dining at ethnic restaurants expanded American taste and diet, improving cultural attitudes, but she recognizes the limits of this in combating long-standing racial prejudice. A large number of experts appear to be shocked that eating ethnic food does *not*, in fact, lead to more favorable attitudes toward immigrants or ethnic minorities but rather is part of an "othering" practice of cultural appropriation and subordination. Whether patrons become better moral actors as a result of dining in unfamiliar places is not an interesting question, in my opinion, because programmed experiences of other cultures, whether through tourism, studying abroad, or eating at foreign restaurants, seldom provide any educational or other beneficial effect. Honeymooning in Cancún or dining in a Mexican restaurant will not necessarily change a person's negative view of Mexican immigrants.

This still leaves open the question of what "normal" American food is. In recent decades, the New American and farm-to-table movements have revived interest in the traditions of American food and certainly made better, fresher, and more artisanal ingredients available. To some extent, the cuisine of such places mimics the eclecticism of ethnic restaurants. Not only are certain ingredients absorbed, but local variation and imitation of other regions (barbecue restaurants in New York, even Texas versus North Carolina barbecue) reproduce the bewildering variety of foreign offerings. There is no agreed-upon background American cuisine. It is neither the international French high-end of the past, nor the equally superseded Jell-O salads and tuna casseroles of the mid-twentieth century. More than anything else, variety and eclecticism characterize the American food scene, for better or worse.

# Cilantro Is Everywhere

## Aralyn Beaumont

We love cilantro. Not every single one of us—some people are wired to perceive the taste of cilantro as soapy—but as a species, we humans are deeply entangled in a symbiotic relationship with *Coriandrum sativum*. We propagate the plant to the tune of hundreds of millions of pounds every year, and in turn, cilantro (aka coriander) brightens and accentuates food everywhere.

Cilantro is as versatile as it is pervasive. You're as likely to find it atop a bowl of soup as on steamed fish or a barbecue-chicken pizza. We blend it into chutney and mince it for salads. We grind the root into a fragrant paste for curries and marinades. We dry the seeds, toast them, and add them to pickle brines and spice mixes like garam masala.

Cilantro leaves and stems energize dishes with the flavors of citrus and pepper and a grassy-piney aroma. They complement sharp, acidic dishes like ceviche, and bring freshness to dark braises and rich meats. We almost always add cilantro immediately before serving, because the plant's volatile flavors can't withstand heat or drying.

The plant originated in the Mediterranean and Middle Eastern regions, then moved to North Africa and India, then on to China and Southeast Asia. Portuguese and Spanish merchants brought it to Mesoamerica. It is an immigrant plant that has affected and improved cuisine wherever it's moved.

Ever the culinary polygamist, cilantro marries equally well with pozole, *kuku sabzi*, and steamed fish.

# We All Want a Good Story

## Luke Tsai

My cousin asked me if it was true that Boston was famous for its pizza. It was the early 2000s, during my second stint as a New England resident, and I had never heard such a thing. This cousin of mine lived in British Columbia, so I just chalked it up to a quaint case of Canadian confusion. Which, in a way, it was—and it wasn't. As it turns out, British Columbia neighbors Alberta, the home base of Boston Pizza, one of Canada's biggest restaurant chains. And Boston Pizza has almost nothing to do with its US namesake.

Of course, there shouldn't be anything surprising about the fact that the name of a restaurant or dish might not be a reliable indicator of its cultural or geographic history. Names, after all, are a kind of story we tell, and sometimes those stories help obscure, mythologize, or straight-up fabricate the true origins of the food we eat.

In the case of Boston Pizza, the real story goes something like this: When a Greek immigrant named Gus Agioritis opened the original Boston Pizza in Edmonton in 1964, he chose the name in part because a young hockey phenom named Bobby Orr was being courted by the Boston Bruins. Being a hockey fan and wanting to instill his restaurant with an aura of American provenance, Agioritis figured "Boston" would make for a fine brand name. The fact that an untold number of Canadians have come of age assuming that

The fictitious origin of Mongolian barbecue nurtures the human proclivity for stories about their food.

Beantown is one of America's great regional pizza hubs is an amusing unintended consequence.

Most of the time, it's the so-called ethnic cuisines (that unwieldy umbrella term used to lump together foods from *somewhere else*) whose names have the most dubious histories. Take crab Rangoon, for instance—a staple of the faux-Polynesian tiki bar and the Chinese American takeout dive. In the early to mid-1900s, Vic Bergeron, the wooden-legged founder of Trader Vic's, started serving fried wontons overstuffed with cream cheese and fake crabmeat. Given the invocation of the colonial-era name of the Burmese capital (now Yangon), you'd be forgiven for thinking the recipe had some basis in an actual Burmese dish. But most evidence indicates that crab Rangoon was Bergeron's own creation. Like most everything else in a tiki bar— the pupu platters, the colorful rum drinks, the kitschy trappings of a faux-Hawaiian luau—the word *Rangoon* serves to convey a whiff of tropical escapism.

And then there's the ubiquitous Chinese chicken salad, which you can find in restaurants as diverse as Applebee's, some Wolfgang Puck establishments, and West Coast Jewish delis. It often appears on menus appended with outlandish names like Mr. Mao's or Asian Chop Chop, harkening back to the days when chop-suey fonts and rampant orientalism were the norm. In a 2017 *New York Times* editorial, Bonnie Tsui writes, "In the ecosystem of the American restaurant menu, the dish checks a box for geographic and flavor diversity outside what company marketers understand to be the norm for their customers. To a white audience, it reads as diverse. To actual Asian-Americans, it reads as ridiculous."

One of the chefs who is often credited with the dish's invention is Cecilia Chiang, California's grande dame of high-end Northern Chinese cooking, who started serving a simple chicken salad at her San Francisco restaurant, The Mandarin, in the early sixties. Chiang says she came up with the salad mostly as a way to use the abundance of leftover iceberg lettuce scraps from her signature minced squab lettuce wraps. She would hand-shred roasted chicken, make a dressing by mixing dry mustard and five-spice powder with neutral-flavored oil, and sprinkle fresh cilantro and crushed peanuts on top.

"Later," Chiang says, "when people copied it, they added all kinds of things," referring to the canned mandarin segments and fried wonton strips that fill out your typical Chinese chicken salad.

Dr. Dan Jurafsky, a linguistics professor at Stanford University,

*Mapo tofu* is named for its alleged inventor: an unnamed woman with a poor complexion.

wrote an entire book, *The Language of Food: A Linguist Reads the Menu*, about the fascinating and often roundabout histories behind run-of-the-mill food words. Jurafsky says that whether you're talking french fries (which were invented in French-speaking Belgium) or hamburgers (after the German city Hamburg), most of the time a country or region that's mentioned in a dish name does play *some* part in the history of that particular food. Even turkey—the animal itself, which traces its zoological and culinary roots to Mexico—got its name because English traders got it confused with a similar-looking African guinea fowl they'd first purchased from the Turkish.

The practice of naming a dish after its creation tale—whether real or imagined—is a universal tendency. In Cape Town, South

The name *spaghetti alla carbonara* (spaghetti in the style of the coal worker) tells us very little about coal workers or the dish.

Africa, the Gatsby sandwich appears to have gotten its name in the 1970s when the owner of a fish-and-chips joint rustled up a sandwich with on-hand ingredients for a few off-duty workers. The monster of a sandwich, overstuffed with bologna, french fries, and *achar*, so satisfied one of the workers, who'd just seen *The Great Gatsby* in theaters, that he called it a "Gatsby smash." In Italy, *spaghetti alla carbonara*—literally, "coal worker's spaghetti"—has been ascribed, variously, to Abruzzian coal miners and to American soldiers who brought their bacon-and-eggs habit overseas during World War II. In China, the clay-encased dish known as beggar's chicken is said to have been invented in ancient times, when a beggar stole a chicken and, lacking a pot, improvised by wrapping the bird in lotus leaves and baking it in mud. *Mapo tofu*, or "pockmarked old lady's tofu," takes its name from the proprietress of a Chengdu restaurant, who, as you may have guessed, was not known for her fair complexion.

Many of these origin tales seem based in some believable history, but sometimes they're completely fabricated. The Italian pasta dish known as puttanesca, for instance, is said to have gotten its "working girl's pasta" designation because it was a flavorful meal that old-timey prostitutes could whip up quickly between sessions. As romantic as that sounds, others believe it's more likely that a chef came up with the name after putting a dish together with *puttanata*, or "garbage," ingredients that he happened to have on hand: tomatoes, olives, capers. Delicious garbage—and nothing to do with sex workers.

In a sense, there's nothing surprising about the fact that people all over the world take these kinds of creative liberties. Cooking and storytelling are, after all, two of the things that make us quintessentially human. We want our food to come from somewhere. All the better if there's a good story behind it that we can talk about while we're sitting around the table. Commerce recognizes this, and gives us what we want.

A lot of what goes into the naming of foods is just a form of marketing. When Jurafsky, the linguist, examined old restaurant menus, he found that for much of the twentieth century, upscale American restaurants tended to insert French words, seemingly at random—"le crabmeat cocktail," "flounder sur le plat," and so forth—as a kind of class marker. Or think of the myriad ways in which a slather of "kimchi mayo" or *gochujang* are translated into nominal Koreanness today: Korean burgers, Korean potato chips, Korean hummus (!).

Viewed charitably, these are just shorthand ways of telling people about what you're cooking. I've always loved the fact that the bakeries and Cantonese barbecue restaurants in Oakland, where I live (and in many other cities with large, intermingled immigrant communities), sell *zong zi*, leaf-wrapped bundles of glutinous rice, as "Chinese tamales"—a nod to their customers' assumed familiarity with Latino food. Similarly, the Ethiopian and Eritrean chickpea dip known as *buticha* is often listed on menus as "Ethiopian hummus," though an Ethiopian friend tells me that when the dish is prepared properly, its texture is closer to that of scrambled eggs.

But in the most egregious instances of externally imposed cultural assignment, there's a certain kind of identity erasure that winds up taking place. One of the most interesting examples is Mongolian barbecue, which most Westerners associate with strip-mall buffet restaurants where a chef stir-fries the diner's choice of meats and vegetables on a round, hibachi-like grill. Often, these restaurants feature Genghis Khan prominently in their decor and offer a history of the cuisine's Mongolian roots. For example, a restaurant in Northern California called Kahunas Mongolian BBQ says this on its website: "Legend has it that after a long day of hunting, Genghis Khan and his Mongolian warriors would make camp and prepare extravagant feasts. Using their swords, the warriors would prepare slivers of meats, combined with whatever vegetables and spices were on hand. They would grill them on their upturned shields over a blazing hot fire."

Of course, none of this has any basis in reality. Dr. Morris Rossabi, a senior scholar and associate adjunct professor of Chinese and Central Asian history, has spent the past several decades studying Mongolian history, and he says he's unaware of any kind of barbecue tradition in Mongolia, where, in his experience, you rarely even see meat and vegetables cooked together in a single dish. There's no evidence that ancient Mongol warriors would slaughter animals for food on the battlefield or that they used their weapons as cooking implements.

The true history of Mongolian barbecue is much more mundane: it was the product of a marketing ploy by Taiwanese restaurateurs in the 1950s. Wu Zhao-Nan, a well-known Chinese comedian who was living in exile in Taipei at the time, is usually credited as the founder of the first Mongolian barbecue restaurant. In a 2013 interview on a Taiwanese news program, he said he'd actually considered naming the style of grilling he created "Beijing barbecue," but in those days such a direct nod to the mainland probably would have gotten some sidelong glances. So Wu settled on calling the new fusion cuisine he'd created "Mongolian barbecue." Because the Mongolian population in Taiwan and the United States, where the restaurants proved to be a hit, was so small, you wound up with a rather unfortunate situation in which the general population had virtually no impression of Mongolian culture apart from this faux-Mongolian restaurant. It didn't help that the restaurants' fictional backstory fed into the stereotype held by some Chinese people that the old Mongolian empire was barbaric and uncultured.

Enkhtuguldur Sukhbaatar, who runs Togi's Mongolian Cuisine in downtown Oakland—one of a small number of true Mongolian eateries in the United States—told me when I reviewed the restaurant in 2016, "I'm not angry. But none of those are really Mongolian." At Togi's, Sukhbaatar serves exceedingly juicy handmade beef dumplings known as *buuz*. To eat one, you first bite a hole in one corner so you can suck out the meaty soup inside. He also serves *tsuivan*, a kind of stir-fry that features hand-cut noodles notable for their chewiness and their crisp-edged char.

One weekend in the spring of 2017, Sukhbaatar invited the local Mongolian community to partake in a rare treat: *khorkhog*, a traditional feast that involves roasting chunks of lamb in a huge jug filled with blazing-hot rocks (or, more often today, in a pressure cooker). After an hour or two, the meat is tender enough to come off the bone, Sukhbaatar says, and the meat juices and rendered fat form a kind of built-in dipping sauce. There can't be more than a handful of restaurants in the United States that serve *khorkhog*. Wouldn't it be something, though, if the dish caught on? Wouldn't it be something if *this* became the new Mongolian barbecue?

As someone who writes about food for a living, I can understand the tendency to choose an evocative dish name over one that's purely descriptive or even strictly historical. After all, it's my job to find the narratives in food—all the ways a collection of ingredients on a plate is more than just the sum of its nutritive parts, and more than something we judge as tasting "good" or "bad." And sometimes a name, all by itself, has the power to transport—whether it's the whimsical imagery of Sichuan Ants Climbing a Tree, or the devilish poetry of the chicken-and-egg dish known as *oyakodon*, i.e. "parent and child in a bowl."

At the end of the day, there's nothing offensive, taste-wise, about many of these creations. A thoughtfully assembled Chinese chicken salad hits the spot on a hot day; at many mediocre chain restaurants, it might be the safest bet on the menu. Even General Tso's chicken—itself the descendent of a dish created by a Taiwanese chef with no connection to any general—deserves its spot in the canon of Chinese American cuisine. These dishes have the potential to hurt when they're promoted in a way that feels exploitative. But they also speak to something else: we all want our food to feel like it came from somewhere. The nice thing is that it all does—sometimes you just have to look beneath the surface. Other times, all you have to do is ask.

# You Can Take the Shoyu Out of Japan

David Zilber

Time and time again, we encounter an ingredient wearing the colors of a country it wasn't born in. Often that ingredient has become so synonymous with its adopted home that its origins are almost lost to history.

But consider what the cooking of Italy would be without the Mesoamerican tomato. What about New Zealand without Eurasian sheep? Or Ireland without the Andean potato?

This is the story of one particularly delicious foodstuff that's been adopted the world over, while never—not for a second—letting people forget where it came from: salty, complex, rich, deep dark soy sauce.

I've never encountered a kitchen cupboard without soy sauce. And one way or another, it's been used on the menu of every restaurant I've ever worked in, save for one: my current employer, Noma. We'll get to that later, but first, let's find out how the liquid runoff of fermented legumes came to conquer the world.

Soy sauce, today mostly sold by gigantic Japanese multinational corporations, hails from ancient China. More than two and a half thousand years ago in eastern China, a parasitic crop fungus was domesticated for its nifty ability to transform everyday staples into a range of wildly delicious comestibles. All of a sudden, with the aid of this fungus, the Chinese were able to turn rice milk into rice wine and soybeans into a slew of nutritious pastes and sauces.

*Aspergillus oryzae* is a fuzzy, sweet-smelling chemical powerhouse of a mold, and an absolutely indispensable agent of fermentation. It produces enzymes that convert starches into simple sugars that can be fermented by yeast into alcohol and break proteins down into amino acids, making foods that are more easily digestible for the intestines and more delicious to the tongue. It grows especially well on grains like rice or barley, in which case it's referred to by its Japanese name, *koji*.

Some of the earliest products of *Aspergillus oryzae* were pastes known as *jiang*s—some of which persist to this day. During the Han dynasty, Chinese cooks prepared these ancient condiments by mixing the mold with salt and cooked soybeans (or meat or fish), and allowing its enzymes to break down the proteins, fats, and starch in a slow fermentative process. As the macromolecules in the soybeans split apart, the liquid that was once bound in the cooked beans was released and pooled on the surface of the ferment. This liquid by-product of soybean *jiang* production was dubbed *jiang you*, which translates quite unpoetically (and less than accurately) to "paste liquid." We know it as soy sauce.

Delicious, packed with nutrition, cellar-stable, and transportable, *jiang*s and *jiang you* went on to define the flavors of cuisines throughout Asia. And preservation through fermentation was further solidified as the means by which the summer's caloric surplus could be stretched out through the off-season, bottled, and stockpiled for when you had more important things to do, like navigate the South China Sea.

Ideas that travel especially well are known as memes. The term was coined by the British ethologist Richard Dawkins in his seminal 1976 work, *The Selfish Gene*. Basically, Dawkins defined a meme as the spread of evolving ideas through human minds in a population, framed in comparison to the spread of genes in a gene pool. Contagious ideas (memes) are said to replace forgettable ones, transmitted by the written or spoken word, and for better or worse, only the most memorable come to survive in the minds and annals of mankind.

Recipes are memes. While soy sauce is a physical thing, it is not one that could exist without the thought process required to brew it. Its taste made it attractive, but the ideas behind it made it valuable and repeatable. Once *jiang*s and *jiang you* reached the rest of Asia, analogs emerged in Indonesia, Vietnam, Thailand, Korea, and, perhaps most notably, Japan, where *jiang*s evolved into misos.

Wheat, a key
component of bread,
pasta, booze, and *shoyu*

*Jiang*s traveled east to Japan from China on the backs of religious emissaries looking to "educate" the Japanese. In Japan, the characters for *jiang you* (酱油) were pronounced as *shoyu*. (*Dou-yu*—a less common Chinese synonym for *jiang you*—translated to *tamari*.)

Along with *jiang*s came the dharmic philosophy of nonviolence, which transformed the island nation's cuisine. In the seventh century, the Japanese emperor Tenmu banned the consumption of all animal meat, except for boar and venison. Though it appears he did so for both utilitarian *and* religious reasons, as Buddhism's influence spread across Japan in the eighth and ninth centuries, the bans on meat consumption grew in scope such that breeding animals for their meat almost completely ceased. The mandates created a void in people's diets and a subsequent shift

toward vegetarian sources of protein: fresh soybeans (edamame), tofu, shoyu, and miso.

Miso making became a national industry, with local varieties reflecting the flavor of their specific regions. Meanwhile, the shoyu that pooled atop wooden buckets of miso grew steadily more coveted—so much so that miso makers began tinkering with ways of increasing the yield of this miso by-product.

In the 1600s, Japanese shoyu makers developed a means of growing *koji* directly on soybeans, mediating moisture content with roasted, cracked wheat. (*Aspergillus oryzae* doesn't like its environment too wet.) In an effort to harvest a purely liquid product, the mixture is submerged in ample amounts of salty brine and left to ferment as a mash known as *moromi*. As such, shoyu became far saltier, and even more shelf-stable, than its pasty progenitor.

Around this time, isolationist Japan was beginning to become a point of interest for the Western world. The German scientist and traveler Engelbert Kaempfer, taking stock of Japan on a two-year voyage in the late 1600s, mentioned shoyu in his treatise *Amoenitatum Exoticarum*. He wrote of a famed sauce called "sooju" made from an unnamed bean. Around the same time, the English physician Samuel Dale published his medical text, *Pharmacologia*, and spoke of the white legume "Japonensium Soia" responsible for a sauce he considered a marked improvement on Chinese ketchups. (Incidentally, these were some of the first instances of the words *sooju* and *soia* ever used in print. The English name "soybean" is derived from the mispronunciation of a condiment so good that it overshadowed its main ingredient.)

Soy sauce was a hot commodity at port, as it traveled extremely well on the long voyages endured by the early trade ships of the burgeoning mercantile era. Conveniently stored at room temperature in nothing more than small wooden barrels, it instantly livened up bland rations. Trade in the sauce soared, and as it spread through the West, soy sauce became an important ingredient in European ferments like Worcestershire sauce (in which it was used until World War II, when it was replaced with cheaper hydrolyzed vegetable protein).

Continuing into the modern era, after World War II, corporations like Kikkoman and Yamasa capitalized on the Western love affair with the umami-rich condiment and marketed it as a new staple for the average American household. Today, soy sauce is the fourth most widely consumed condiment in the States.

Soy sauce penetrated every level of Western cooking, including the uppermost echelons. In 1978, the late, great chef Alain Senderens, inspired by a recent trip to China, sent the Parisian dining scene into a panic when he began adding soy sauce to the beurre blanc at his three-Michelin-star restaurant.

Perhaps Senderens met such friction because he made a point of *telling* his guests that he was using soy sauce. When applied in the right quantities, soy sauce elevates dishes. The tricky thing is that those quantities have to remain below the radar, lest diners immediately identify the flavor as "Asian." As flavorful an ingredient as soy sauce is, it's dwarfed by its immense power as a cultural icon.

In linguistics, *indexicality* describes the mind's ability to link a word to the context of its occurrence. For example, reading the word *smoke* immediately generates thoughts and images of burning candles and campfires. When you read *shoyu*, you think Japanese food.

Zooming out a level, indexicality defers to a larger branch of study called semiotics, which examines the production and meaning of signs. Semiotics deals with linguistic and nonlinguistic signs, and the meaning that comes from all forms of sensory input—smell and taste included. If the word *smoke* makes us think of fire, the smell of smoke does so to an even greater extent.

This link between sense and meaning kept our ancestors alive for millennia. It is encoded directly into our genome, expressed as our perception of flavor. We are wired to be wary of bitter or sour tastes, as they're often indicative of poison. On the other hand, our bodies tell us to gorge on the energy-rich likes of fats and sugars, which not coincidentally, taste good. Just thinking about smelling rotting, putrid roadkill decaying in the hot sun can trigger nausea. On the other hand, a warm smile might break out when you recall the intoxicatingly sweet smell of apple pie baking in Mom's oven.

We think about the connection between taste and memory constantly at Noma, where I work as the sous-chef in charge of fermentation. When the restaurant opened in 2003, it set out to describe the flavors of the Nordic region. The Nordics, while not devoid of a cultural food history in any sense, were hard-pressed to define it, let alone celebrate it. And so, the team set out to eschew the traditions of haute cuisine and forge a new identity by delving into the region's history and landscape with a specific set of limitations: they would only use products from the region.

"Self-imposed restriction brings focus," said the physicist Dr. John D. Barrow, and it is intensely true for Noma. By limiting their view to Scandinavian ingredients, the Noma staff were obliged to look farther afield for techniques that could help breathe new life into familiar raw products. They found particular inspiration in the biological decoder ring that is fermentation.

Techniques that were thousands of years old became novel when applied to Nordic inputs, yielding a plethora of tastes that felt brand-new, yet distinctly of this place. The full-on embrace of fermentation transformed Noma's cooking, spurred on new fields of research, and even bore a lab dedicated to its exploration, to which I owe my employment.

Every door we open in the fermentation lab yields more questions, more paths to follow. One striking success that's become a pillar of Noma's menu is peaso—our adaptation of Japanese miso. In our version, peas—a high-protein legume endemic to northern Europe—takes the place of the soybean, and our *koji* is grown on Danish barley in lieu of rice. The first batch blew our minds. It was an extension of a celebrated meme, but it didn't *taste* of Asia the way that, say, crème brûlée always tastes of France no matter if it's flavored with vanilla beans or sea buckthorn.

Naturally, we chased this line of thinking down the rabbit hole, testing out different legumes, ratios, and flavorings to see what stuck. At one point, our line of inquiry brought us face-to-face with shoyu. Following classical Japanese methodology, we made our own

Cedar barrels known as *kioke* are used for fermenting.

shoyu, again swapping in yellow peas for soybeans and barley for rice. The result? Delicious. After about six months of fermentation, we pulled the first batches and found them to be amazing. They rivaled some of the best artisanal shoyus we'd had the pleasure of tasting when we did the Noma pop-up in Tokyo.

I recall a cold January day, when a good friend of the restaurant, Shinobu Namae (chef and owner of L'Effervescence in Tokyo), was touring our facilities. We pushed a sample of our virgin brew on him.

"Yup, that's shoyu," he announced.

It was a compliment, but one I've come to realize carried a weight that can't easily be shaken off.

You see, for all the liters and varieties of Nordic shoyu we've produced since then, none has ever managed to make its way into a Noma recipe. Every time a chef in the test kitchen—where the restaurant's dishes are conceived and tinkered with—uses a splash of shoyu to add depth to a sauce or saltiness to a marinade, the trial is inevitably scrapped. But why?

Though we've dramatically loosened our restrictions on regionality, Noma is still a restaurant that expends enormous amounts of energy to convey a narrative of time and place, using the semiotics of food to achieve its ends. Without fail, Nordic shoyu jarringly knocks our guests out of this narrative, transporting them instantly from their sheepskin-lined chairs in a quiet corner of Copenhagen to a neon-lit alleyway on a boisterous Tokyo side street.

No one issues passports for ideas. When you return from a trip abroad, the customs agent doesn't ask you to declare what valuable memories of flavors and smells you're bringing home. There are no Homeland Security agents to stop you from cooking an inspired rendition of the *bucatini all'amatriciana* you had last spring in Rome. And we should all be thankful for that.

We are all free to try to produce soy sauce wherever we are in the world, for soy sauce isn't merely a slew of organic chemicals suspended in an ionic solution; it's an ongoing history thousands of years long and billions of individuals strong. It weaves a thread through the traditional cuisines of at least a half dozen countries without giving a damn about borders.

Every time you taste it brushed over *nigiri*, wok-fried into *nasi goreng*, or grilled into *bulgogi*, it is direct in its announcement not only of what you're tasting, but when and where you first tasted it. There is no need to buy a ticket to return to the memories of the best times of your life. The semiotics of taste have a powerful hold on our memories, informed by the accumulation of all our uncountable life experiences. Thus, for the vast majority of us, the taste of soy sauce is intractably linked to Asia.

So was our effort to produce a Nordic soy sauce a failure?

Absolutely not—only by crossing into other lands do we learn something about ourselves and the world at large. At Noma, Nordic shoyu will remain a concoction that, as delicious as it may be, cannot transcend the cultural weight of the region that first produced it. Our tests will stay shelved, aging and improving, as curious experiments that taught a valuable lesson about the interface of heritage and flavor.

And to our hypothetical culinary customs agent, I say, "Yes, sir, I've got something to declare."

# Coffee Saves Lives

**Arthur Karuletwa**

**as told to Chris Ying**

My name is Arthur Karuletwa. I'm the director of Global Coffee Traceability and Origin Experience for Starbucks.

I'm Rwandese by nationality, but usually if somebody asks me where I'm from, I'll just say I'm from California.

"But you have an accent," they'll say.

"I've traveled a lot."

It's a white lie. But the truth always ends up coming back to bite me, and that's why I lie. I'm selfishly avoiding getting upset or offended.

I can't tell you how many times I've told someone I'm from Rwanda, and the person says, "Where's that?" or "Is there still war there?" or "Are you okay?"

I've even gotten the question directly: "Aren't you from Rwanda?" And I say, "No."

Back when I was in college, my mentor, Gary, wanted to pay for me to go to counseling. He decided my story was just too insane, that I needed to talk to someone. Because I was new to the country, I mostly said yes to things.

The therapist's first question was, "So where are you from? Are you from Africa?"

"Yes, Rwanda."

He goes, "Where is that?"

Bless his heart, he was probably good at psychology and understanding people's traumatic situations—how to speak to them and how to pull them out of it. But I was very fatigued by the idea of educating him about who I am, where I'm from, the people there.

After the first day, Gary would drop me off for therapy and I wouldn't go in. I would just keep walking. When I ended up admitting it to him, I said, "I can't talk to a stranger about my problems. I need to talk to a relative or somebody who went through it, too. If they've successfully overcome the bitterness or pain, or what it is that is making me angry, I'd love to hear what they did. But where am I going to find them?"

He felt horrible, and he said, "I don't know what to tell you, Arthur, but from my experience, when I have an issue with someone or something, I carry out what I call a historical process of elimination. I go back to find what triggered the issue—that way I know how to deal with it."

In simple terms: deal with your past, so you can understand how to move on.

I was born in 1975 in Uganda, near the Rwandan border.

Lots of people remember the Rwandan Genocide from 1994, but before then, every ten years there were pockets of many killings, atrocities, and other reasons for Tutsis—the ethnic group of which I am a part—to flee Rwanda. The conflict between Tutsis and Hutus—Rwanda's majority ethnic group—goes back generations, based on a long history of fear promoted by French and Belgian colonists who pitted one race against another. My parents' generation fled in the seventies, only to be introduced to the war between Idi Amin and Milton Obote in Uganda, causing us to flee yet again to Kenya when I was two years old.

I was raised in Kenya until I was about eleven years old. It was in Kenya where we first had what I'd call a normal life, but we worked hard to fit in with our surroundings. My dad's voice always comes to mind, talking about why we were dressing a certain way, why we were speaking with a certain accent, or why we weren't eating certain foods. My dad wanted us to blend in. "You need to learn Swahili, you need to have a Kenyan accent. Dress like they dress, eat like they eat, talk like they talk, to reduce any friction."

My brothers and sister and I are all two years apart—close enough to be able to hang out and do things together. And because we moved so much, we were both related and best friends. I remember having this realization where I thought, *I just called my brother my best friend. That's not right. I want an unrelated best friend!*

My dad worked his butt off. He was in the transportation business. We barely saw him because he was always working, driving his trucks, transporting goods between borders from as far away as Congo—Goma, Kisangani—through Burundi, Tanzania, Uganda. He did the East African roads all the way to the port of Mombasa and Dar es Salaam. He transported everything from rice and flour from the United Nations Food and Agriculture Organization to US cooking oil to coffee for private businesses.

He drove really old beater trucks, and the roads he took were extremely bad and dangerous. He would sometimes spend months away. A trip from Goma to Mombasa would take five months—if the car broke down, add another month. The irony is that he was going through countries that we were running from. I remember we'd all ask my mom, "If Dad can go there, why can't we?" I learned that there's a lot of money in countries in turmoil. There's a lot of wealth in war, so to speak.

When I was eleven, we moved back to Uganda, because it was really hard being in Kenya, being a Rwandan from Uganda. A lot of my dad's efforts to run a business were foiled. I felt like everywhere we went, we were trying to participate in the economy and trying to participate in school. Never once did I see or hear my dad cheat or try to take somebody else's property or do something illegal, despite the fact that we were in survival mode. Sometimes when you get to that point, desperation makes you do things. I never saw my father get there, but it was always a struggle.

Through his work, he had developed relationships with some of the leaders in the Ugandan National Resistance Army. He helped move some critical ammunition for them. In fact, he played such a key role that when they won the war, the new president, Yoweri Museveni, publicly gave him a medal. He felt like he was being embraced and that we should probably go and see what other opportunities there were in Uganda.

Museveni had just taken over. We basically moved in right behind the rebel battalion as the capital city was being taken. There were still bodies in the streets. Bullet shells everywhere. One of my brothers was killed when someone threw a grenade into a crowd of people he happened to be standing in. Another brother was there, and when he heard the blast, he started running and just kept running. That's how fresh everything was in postwar Uganda at the time.

We went to school and everyone acted normal, but for three or four years, there wasn't a night that there weren't gunshots in the air—sometimes in the far distance, sometimes closer. It was still the Wild West. There was nothing normal about it, but we acted like it was, because we so badly wanted normal.

In Uganda, now we had to be Ugandan. We had to dress Ugandan, eat Ugandan. There are sixteen different dialects in Uganda. We learned four of them. At fifteen, I protested to my parents, "Let's go back home"—"home" meaning Kenya.

At that age, I resented being in Uganda, and my brothers and I were very rebellious about it. My parents sent us to boarding school because of it—not that I blame them.

Everywhere we went, we were seeking to blend into this foreign identity that wasn't ours. When we finally got the chance to go to Rwanda, it felt almost like stripping your clothes off and saying, "Here I am, the true self, the whole me," and embracing your own identity. Finally, we thought, we wouldn't have to fake it anymore.

We were keeping a close eye on the peace talks in Rwanda, which began as soon as we got to Uganda in 1990. There was talk of a potential election and the possibility for Tutsis to come back home.

Lo and behold, in 1993 in Arusha, Tanzania, the president of Rwanda signed a peace treaty with the Rwandese Patriotic Front, and we were heading home. We started packing our stuff and at the end of '93 began heading out there.

As we started leaving, the president was on his way back to Rwanda when his plane was shot down. It is alleged that some members of his parliament felt betrayed that he had signed a treaty with the enemy, and were complicit in the crash. Regardless, that's when the strategic and very timely genocide began. The president's plane was still in flames when the roadblocks went up and the machetes came out. They had distributed machetes and handheld radios all over the country weeks earlier. My dad called his brother to find out what happened. "We've heard there was a plane crash. What's going on?"

My dad's brother, who was already in the country, said, "It's the president's plane. They've taken it down and it is intentional and all hell is breaking loose. Turn around now."

My dad left to go see if he could save his brother, if he could save his other family members, my uncles, my aunts, my grandparents who were in the country. Meanwhile, we hunkered down. We didn't see him for a long time.

My mom would be on the phone with relatives and suddenly hear people saying, "They're at the door. I have to go." Some of them would not even hang the phone up. They would just leave it up there and my mom could hear the mutilation, just complete anarchy.

My older brothers ran away in the night to go fight with the army. My mom was part of a women's group that was cooking meals, helping those who had gotten injured or those who were lost. Because my mom held such a significant role at the women's group, she was always given the courtesy of being notified when one of her boys had run away to fight. She'd always try and convince one of the army personnel to send him back home.

When the fighting began, I thought at first that it was like every other war I had witnessed. But I soon realized that this one was different. This one had fewer guns and grenades and standard— Western-style annihilation apparatus. It was a meticulous process carried out with machetes.

Your appearance became your death warrant. The main physical differences between Tutsis and Hutus—Rwanda's ethnic majority— is that Hutus are shorter and dark skinned and sturdier in their physique. Tutsis are taller, lankier, and light skinned.

It didn't matter what you said. If you looked Tutsi, they would kill you. People claimed to be the children of rape by Tutsis so that they might be spared, but no one was buying it. The way you looked determined whether you lived or died. A million people died in a hundred days. That's ten thousand people each day.

My dad's brother stayed in Rwanda. He vowed he was going to die there. He would not run anymore. He had his family with him in the house when the militia came to the door. He sent his wife and four boys to the back of the house, and he opened the door and said, "There's no one here but me. I know you're here for me. So where do you want to do this?" They came in and found his family anyway.

My uncle paid them everything—his car, all their money, whatever jewelry they had—hoping the mercenaries would shoot them rather than cut them down with machetes. The mercenary with a gun held up a bullet and said, "Do you know what this is made out of? This is copper. Do you know how much copper costs? I'm not going to waste my copper on you. What else have you got?" My uncle gave them everything they wanted.

Their last request was his wife. Six men raped her in front of her husband and children. The mercenaries left her for dead, and still macheted my uncle and cousins, but she survived. She's the only one still alive. She tells us this story. It's one of a million stories like it.

Later, after the last machete was put down and we took a look around, we thought, *What were they fighting for?* The country barely has any natural resources—no oil, no minerals. It's a very agrarian economy. Rwanda is small, and land is a huge resource.

Everybody was very poor. It wasn't as if there was any sense of pride of heritage and culture that was worth fighting for, either. It wasn't even clearly defined who and what you were meant to be proud of. In other places, like Sudan, there are incredible resources like oil that people are willing to kill for. There's a sense that *This will be our lifeline should we win this battle.* The genocide in Rwanda was based on a long history of fear of the other side, beginning with the French and Belgians favoring one race over another and ensuring that that race would maintain control of territorial Rwanda.

The Belgians began by educating the Tutsis in the early twentieth century, but that led to demands for democracy and independence. And so the colonists turned the Tutsis away and told the Hutus, "You are the majority tribe here. *You* should rule Rwanda instead—as long as you don't ask a lot of questions."

For decades, there had been propaganda circulating among the Hutus against the Tutsis and vice versa. The Hutus talked about how Tutsis would return to take Hutu jobs and Hutu property. They had all these sayings and poems. There was a list of ten commandments: *Thou shall not do business with a Tutsi. Thou shall not eat at the same table or break bread with a Tutsi.* And so on and so forth.

One saying that they taught from a small age was spoken with almost a melody to it: *When the forest starts to encroach on your area, equip yourself with a machete and cut its branches down.*

It's disturbing that in this age and time, we are still hearing similar things all around the world. I always try to consider whose mouths those words are coming from, and what their background and motivation are. People's background and motivation define how they weigh their worth and the worth of others.

———

I think one of my saving graces was that I left Rwanda a year after the genocide, at Christmas in 1995. I wanted to stay, because I didn't want to leave my mom, and I didn't know where my dad was yet. I didn't see my dad again until 2001. I had friends who went to battle and died, and my brother who'd been killed by a land mine. I thought, *How dare I go get my education in America while everybody else has sacrificed for me to do this?* There was guilt, shame, and anger.

Before I left, we were living in Rwanda's capital, Kigali, in an abandoned house. When we arrived, we just picked any house. The beds and furniture were still there, unmoved.

It smelled like death everywhere. It smelled bad for a long time. The river ran red with blood, bodies everywhere, bloodstains on walls of churches.

Our moments of happiness were when we'd all huddle around a candle—there were days when electricity was rationed and we had no power—and reminisce about people we knew and what they used to say or how they used to make us feel. Sometimes we'd go play soccer out in the back, or we'd play basketball at the military camp in the evenings.

I loved basketball. It's the one thing that I did that made me forget what was going on around me. I had a knack for it, too. When we were in Uganda, there was a coach from Oxnard College, in California, doing a basketball camp in Kampala. He was really interested in my coming over to the States on a scholarship and developing my game. But that was when I was seventeen or eighteen, a year before my family left for Rwanda. By the time he reached out to the embassy in Uganda to find out where I was, my basketball team said, "He's moved back to Rwanda."

When he tried to contact the embassy in Rwanda, it was shut down. Fortunately, they reopened the embassy with Rwandan staff and one American employee who had refused to leave during the genocide. Coach Virgil Watson was dead set on finding me. I think he knew what was happening in the country and had made it a personal mission.

I wasn't going to go. But my mom, in her mellow yet deliberate style, said to me, "You think that by staying here you're doing me a favor?"

I said, "Mom, I will never leave you."

She said, "Well, every time you walk out that door, whether you're going to go play basketball or meet your friend or I send you for milk, I die a small death. My heart's getting weaker and weaker every time, because I don't believe you're coming back. If you want to resuscitate me, you better go make all these lives that we've just lost not in vain. Survive for a reason and go prove why. If you think you're saving me, go."

So I came to America.

In Los Angeles, my brother picked me up from the airport and drove me straight to my first restaurant in America. I'll never forget it: Black Angus. He told me I would love the ribs. He said, "You must be hungry. Get a full rack."

When the ribs arrived, I thought they'd killed an antelope or something. There was so much food. My brother was going to town on the bones, and I'm just like, *I'm so hungry, but I don't know if I can eat this.* I ate all the bread I could eat and just left the meat there.

I thought of what my dad used to say every time we moved from one place to another. "If you don't fit in, you will be noticed, and we'll be in trouble, so for crying out loud, fit in." I wanted to fit in, but I was a zombie. I barely spoke to anyone. I could go for a week without saying a word, not even to ask for the ball to be passed to me on the court.

There was a multitude of ethnicities and cultures and religions and differences in America. I thought, *Which one am I going to gravitate to?* Ninety percent of my basketball team was African American, but I didn't feel like I understood them, nor did they seem to understand me. What they were dealing with was completely different from what I was dealing with. Caucasians loved to hear about where I was from and weren't shy about asking questions—right or wrong, they just said what they said. I was also in a very large demographic of Mexicans. My best friend was a Mexican guy. The way I identified with him was that the only food I could eat for a long time was rice and beans, so he was my best friend for that reason. I knew that he knew the good spots.

I lived on campus at Ventura College during the school year. Every basketball player had a mentor assigned to them, and in the summer I lived with my mentor, Gary, who was the dean of history. He pretty much became my dad away from home. He was an older white guy with a big beard—he looked like Santa Claus. We had nothing in common, yet everything in common. He loved history, loved knowing and learning about different cultures. We would stay up forever talking about my experience and where I was from, and he would talk to me about American history and all kinds of stuff. I owe him a lot for helping me start to live again.

His house was in this place called Ojai, which probably had a black population of one. It was in the middle of nowhere, with orange trees all around the place, and it was super hot, but it was fine. It gave me the space to really process everything, to read a lot, because I really wanted to understand how the heck what had happened had happened.

I did not know how people could slaughter themselves to this degree. Yes, I had heard about the colonial days. I had heard about measuring people's noses, height, and skin color, and defining them as a Tutsi or a Hutu. I read about French colonialists saying that, "Because you have the frame and skin tone of a white male, you must be smarter than this darker-skinned person, so we'll favor you." I heard all that stuff, read all that stuff, but it still wasn't enough justification for me, based on what I had witnessed.

My mom's words kept ringing in my head: *Go make all these lives that we've just lost not in vain.* And that's all I focused on. I did not know how I was going to achieve it. I couldn't bring them back to life, and I didn't know how to revive Rwanda from the depths it was in. I battled and struggled with that statement—I almost felt trapped by it. I even tried to shake it off. At one point, I accused my mom of not being in the right frame of mind when she said those words, because she couldn't possibly have understood their impact.

Gary told me that I needed to follow the history of why I was bitter, angry, and vengeful. I decided to read everything I could in even more depth. Maybe I'd missed something about colonization. Maybe I'd missed something about the Hutu-Tutsi feud. I read all kinds of books about the history of my people, the history of the entire region and migration of the Bantus, and Nilotics, and Semites, and so on. I read analysts' white papers, so-called regional experts' white papers.

None of it really resonated with me; it wasn't what I was looking for. None of it loosened the choke hold I was feeling. I couldn't find any solace.

So I brushed it all aside, and like an epiphany, I decided, *You know what? I am my best witness. I was there. I saw it all and I heard it all. I still feel it.* I decided that if I thought hard enough, long enough, deep enough, I could come up with my own hypothesis as to how a million people could be wiped off the face of the planet in a matter of days.

———

I'd moved from junior college to a four-year college called the Master's University in Santa Clarita, California. I started reading theology, and through that whole process, through a lot of thought process, I started to understand the things I had seen.

The conclusion I came to was that I had witnessed the worst form of poverty. And I began to define poverty in two ways. One, being the standard Webster's dictionary or economics-lecture-room definition: the lack of availability of basic needs, like water, food, shelter—all tangible things. But there is another kind of poverty that has more to do with the impoverishment of the human soul and the human spirit. It is the lack of identity.

We revere our identity. Every day we wake up thinking about maintaining a polished identity, because that's our core of empowerment. That's where we derive our ability to open a bank account, get a driver's license, get a paycheck, be recognized. From the moment you are born and given a birth certificate, you're building the foundation of who you are as a person.

It's hard to fathom that more than a billion people on earth have no such way to identify themselves. Not having identity or self-worth makes you invisible. It makes you less than human. The poverty that is internal leads you to self-destruction. That's the one I really started to dig into, and I saw every Rwandan—mostly Hutus—falling into that category. And I could apply it to other places that are going through similar atrocities. If you have self-worth, you have a better chance to see and sustain a road map to achieve what in Rwanda we call *agaciro*, a cultural identity.

Once I had this realization, I felt tremendous emotional relief. Approaching graduation, I continued to have these aha moments, where I was beginning to zero in on exactly what I wanted to do, where I wanted to do it, and how I wanted to do it. I needed to tackle poverty—both economic and spiritual.

I began trying to understand poverty eradication tactics— things that have been tried everywhere by the private sector and the public sector, development agencies, and everything in between. I looked at the economic and social indices around what determines when someone categorizes themselves as poor or impoverished. The social index meant a lot more to me than the economic index, but I knew that the first domino was the economics.

Rwanda revolves around agriculture. Tutsis were traditionally pastoralists, so we tended to cattle, goats, and chickens—animal husbandry. A lot of the Hutus tilled the soil. They grew bananas, potatoes, carrots. We traded that way—milk for honey, cowhides for potatoes, etc.

And when I looked at the cash crops, coffee and tea stood out as the backbone of the economy. Predating the wars and genocide, it's always been coffee and tea.

Commodity products lack intimacy. In general, people have very little regard for who's growing their rice or beans.

But when you're talking about specialty products like cheese or chocolate or coffee, there's a more refined demand for granularity about the product and where it came from—the place, the culture, the growing conditions, even the carbon footprint. All of that is very relevant and important. And therein lie the nuggets of who the growers are. That's why I decided to pursue coffee over tea. Coffee was going to be my number one agent in my war on poverty.

Every rural Rwandan grew coffee. The first trees came from the island of Bourbon and were planted by French missionaries. That's why the Bourbon variety is predominant in Rwanda.

Coffee in Rwanda had three rules back in the colonial days. Rule number one, established by the Belgians, was that every Rwandan who had property that was conducive to growing coffee had to grow coffee. It didn't matter how small your property was—if it was within a certain distance from the city, you had to grow it.

The second law was that you couldn't cut down a coffee tree without permission. You were not to damage or cut down a coffee tree, or grow anything that would suffocate the coffee plant.

The third law was that you were not to consume coffee, or use it in any way.

They even did test runs where they brought coffee to farmers and communities and said, "We'll give you a small dose to show you that this will kill you if you take it in large doses." Thanks to the caffeine rush, people's hearts would start beating fast and they would say, "Oh my God, this will kill us. It's a Western medicinal product."

I read all about this in college, where I would do my homework in Starbucks stores and different coffee shops around town. I saw how much coffee excited people, how much people convened around it. It could be a business meeting, a marriage proposal, a birthday—you name it. It was always, "Let's meet for coffee." It was very intriguing for me that coffee was the point of connection.

Coffee is only grown in very specific places around the world. Every single morning, the very first thing we do is connect with this world that none of us think about. That's our first act of the day. Hundreds of millions of kitchen counters have a portal into a world people can't believe or imagine. Because of coffee, I can introduce a woman and three children here in Seattle, Washington, to a woman with two children in the middle of nowhere in Rwanda. I can create a sense of familiarity and thereby a sense of empathy.

Even back then, I liked to call coffee the loudest yet voiceless refugee. It comes to the land of abundance from countries that are at war, considered hostile, impoverished, lacking opportunity. People can barely pronounce the name on the bag, but because it sounds exotic, unique, different, rare, they're excited, like, "I tried this coffee from this unknown place."

After college, I went straight to work for a company called the Green Room in Auburn, Washington. They're a warehouse that stores green coffee. There were days when I unloaded ten containers of coffee—two hundred burlap bags each. I palletized them and learned how to ride a forklift (and tore a lot of bags in the meantime).

I wanted to understand how coffee comes into the country as a raw natural product. It was fascinating work because I was the first point of connection to the coffee from the outside world—the first person to open that door and welcome the coffee from its long journey as a refugee.

From the Green Room, I then went to work for Millstone Coffee. I wanted to understand every part of the value chain of coffee. Before they were acquired by Procter & Gamble, Millstone Coffee used to roast their own coffee on Bainbridge Island, in Washington, and distribute it in grocery stores. My next step after Millstone would have been to work in a store, but I didn't get the chance, because an opportunity came up in the Ministry of Agriculture in Rwanda. They were looking to hire somebody to help them build up their coffee industry from a value, marketing, and branding standpoint.

This was in 2001 or 2002. I cut short my journey of understanding coffee on the market side and ran for that opportunity. My boss at Millstone said, "What are you doing? We see you as a promising candidate in this company. Why don't you take a leave of absence? If things don't go as planned, you can always come back."

I looked him in the eye and told him, "You have to let me quit.

If I don't quit, if I know there's a safety net, I'll be fine with falling. I have to know there's nothing."

I hadn't been back to Rwanda since I'd left for school six or seven years earlier, and it took me about eight months to prepare for the leap of faith I was about to take. One of the most difficult things I needed to process was knowing that 98 percent of the coffee farmers in Rwanda are Hutu.

If I was being true to my measure of social impact and goal of leveraging coffee as a piece of reconciliation, then I had to accept that I was walking into the lion's den. I was going to look the enemy in the eye and say, "I'm here to reconcile, I'm here to embrace, I'm here to make sure what happened in '94 never happens again."

I needed to forgive and reconcile without expecting reciprocation.

Rwanda was liberalizing the coffee market. They were creating an environment where you could grow coffee, you could cut the trees, you could grow whatever you wanted. While liberalizing the market, they also wanted to create an emphasis on why coffee was important to the economy.

They wanted to turn the industry from commodity-driven coffee into specialty coffee, without really understanding that it's not just about improving the quality. There's a lot that defines specialty coffee. You could have a fantastic-tasting cup of coffee, but nobody's going to buy it if you don't have any transparency about where it came from or who paid for it, or if it's coming from a conflict-ridden region and potentially supporting an oppressive regime, or if it damaged the environment during its production or its processing. There are so many components that go into establishing a coffee as specialty coffee, not just how it tastes. All of those things require a human force to establish.

So I banged on the minister of agriculture's door and said, "I'm the one who has been e-mailing you back and forth. I'm here for the job."

He looked at me and said, "I could tell from your last name that you were Rwandan, but now that I see you in person—do you realize what you're signing up for?"

"Yes."

He goes, "No, you don't."

He hadn't realized over e-mail that I was Tutsi. He thought the job would be suicide. He sent me away: "I don't want to be responsible for an employee going missing. I'll get arrested. The government will ask me what I was thinking. No."

The president of Rwanda had spent some time in the United States and in the United Kingdom speaking to the young Rwandan diaspora in exile, saying, "Your country needs you now. We are working on stabilizing security, creating an environment of investment, and getting back normalcy. We need your great, young minds." His talks moved me to persist, and eventually the minister hired me as a consultant, warning me again about what I was about to face.

I had spent eight months preparing for those kinds of statements, preparing to face a group of coffee farmers from the opposite ethnic group and talk to them about why I was there. But what threw me a curveball was my experience with my own ethnic group. I thought they would understand my motivation for economic reconciliation, but instead, I experienced critical skepticism.

They were right to be angry, to feel like I was not prioritizing their needs but rather what was perceived to be our mutual enemy's needs. For me to come to the country and go straight to the rural sector to work with the perpetrators of the genocide, I was viewed as relieving the perpetrators before those whom they had tormented.

I told them I had to be selfish before I could be selfless. This is the method I had chosen, and they had to respect it. I didn't expect them to accept it, but I pleaded with them to respect it in the short run. If it didn't pan out, then I'd made the dumbest mistake I'd ever made, and I was willing to live with that. I headed for the fields.

The minister had given me three challenging co-ops to deal with: one that was run by women, one that was struggling to make ends meet, and one that had just gotten a new president because the last one was in prison for corruption. And on top of building the value chain, I had to build a market strategy and represent the co-ops at different trade shows. And on top of *that*, I was a young guy starting a new job. I could have worn a T-shirt that read WHAT AM I DOING? That's where I started.

At my first cooperative meeting, I was supposed to introduce myself, spend some time with their leadership and their agronomists and their farmers in the field. Start to develop some basics on how we were going to build value around their product.

I was the only one who spoke for two days. "Anyone have any questions?" No. "Can we introduce ourselves?" Nothing.

I put all my books away, all my notebooks, my laptop, and I decided I was going to dedicate a month to getting to know them and letting them get to know me. I broke bread with them, talked to them about business, how they're selling their lettuce and their carrots, talking to their kids, rolling in the dirt, playing soccer in the fields. Basically, I immersed myself in the community.

For them to see me eat their food was significant, because there were incidents happening in the countryside where Tutsi domestic workers were being poisoned at restaurants run by Hutus. For me to eat with them was huge. It showed I was willing to risk death for them.

I'd go to places where cell phone bars were nonexistent and my car was six miles away. They could've done away with me at any moment. But I didn't feel scared until I saw the machetes, the tool of mutilation. When I saw the tool, it became real. Something about the tool, something about the way they used it to cut branches off trees, the way they weeded the earth, the way they chopped things with vigor, just didn't sit well with me. I didn't see that one coming. I wasn't sure I would be able to do this.

In the fifteen and a half years I've been working in Rwanda, I've worked many times with people who took part in the genocide. I've engaged with people who participated in the killings of my own family.

As I was trying to create trust between myself and the farmers, they were experiencing distrust among themselves.

At a table of ten farmers, someone's quality would be horrible, another's fantastic. His trees look old, she's growing bananas next to hers, he has an insect problem. Yet the mind-set was that we were all going to pool together and sell our coffee. There's a saying in Rwandan that is pretty equivalent to "one bad apple spoils the basket" in English. They were quick to understand that, but no one was ready to call out the bad apples.

There's a trust factor at work. We worked on that. We worked on accountability. We worked on incentivizing.

I looked through the products and said, "All these cherries are green and infested with insects. Look at these other cherries— beautiful, red, plump, not damaged. Why should I buy these two cherries for the same price?"

Rather than mixing everything together just to get the volume up, we incentivized quality. Quality over quantity was a notion that was foreign to them. We had to reverse the ingrained thinking of low quality, high volume. And it was difficult to tell them, "I know you just carried sixty kilos of cherries on your head for an hour to get here, but you're going to have to carry them back."

There was a huge conversation around pride and self-worth. Small quantities of high-quality coffee are more valuable, in the sense of financial reward but, more important, in terms of recognition. I could tell people were excited about the recognition. "Out of three thousand people, your coffee is fantastic—here's a bonus. And can I send an agronomist to your farm so that you can become a farmer-trainer?" We'd get people to go and see the better farms, train, and help out. I saw firsthand people coming just to get recognized.

There were angry people, too. They were angry that we were training the managers at the wet mills to reject berries below a certain quality. We ended up creating a program where they wouldn't have to take their coffee back, but it wouldn't go into the basket with the quality coffee. It would be sorted and processed separately. It would go to another client to be put in tin cans. And it wouldn't be labeled "Rwandan coffee."

Slowly, you began to see people's disappointment become less about the money they were losing and more about being segregated. When your work goes into the big pool with everyone else's, your identity is diluted. It was that social-index component that they found hard to move on from.

Rwanda is the only country where the category of smallholder farm is even further divided into micro-farmers. Eighty percent of the global supply of coffee comes from smallholders. The other 20 percent comes from farmers who own estates. The size for a smallholder is somewhere between one thousand and twenty-five hundred trees. In Rwanda, you've got people with two hundred trees, or fifty, or twenty. With micro-farmers, the level of competition is extremely high, and your ability to control quality is extremely fickle.

To me, that meant Rwanda was the perfect landscape to say, "I know traceability is already a foundational principle of safety standards and tracking items that could potentially cause illnesses. But we're going to use it here to maintain and preserve people's identity—not the product, but the people."

After two years, I was asked to be the coffee strategist at the national coffee board. I worked until 2008 on the value chain, marketing and branding Rwandan coffee. I built roaster-retail stores and a traceability system. We built out the process, where we were able to look at a container of coffee and know who the contributors were, and what day, what time, and where they had contributed. All those things happened while I was there.

I was building retail stores and consulting as a strategist when Starbucks was going through a PR crisis in Ethiopia. There was a trademark issue where Ethiopia was claiming that Starbucks and others were selling coffee under names like Sidamo, Harar, and Yirgacheffe without paying for the use of those names. As a matter of fact, the industry really brought to light the value of these names through their marketing. That being said, Ethiopia wanted to trademark these geographical locations. They hired intellectual property lawyers and everything.

But the only way to leverage those geographic indications is if you can guarantee that the coffee is actually coming from these places. You have to be willing to govern and control the process of verifying where the coffee is coming from. And you need to be able to show the roasters and the customers that this system you're going to build will allow for transparency and will be the driver of a repeatable and sustainable business, make their work easier, and be a continuous incentive for them to buy more from you. They need to feel that you are assisting in maintaining quality and validation so that they are protected as a brand. If they chose to put "Sidamo" on the bag and pay you for it, they need to see what value that brings them.

The attorneys representing Ethiopia wrote a petition to the National Coffee Association, which is a coffee trade association in the United States. That year happened to be the year an executive from Starbucks was serving as the governing member of the board—a position that rotates every two years. The whole board rejected the petition and suggested that certification was more probable than trademarking geographical indications. But because it was a Starbucks executive in charge at the time, the news headlines were all about Starbucks rejecting Ethiopia's efforts to protect their geographic identities.

In the meantime, we were busy certifying regions in Rwanda. All the while, Starbucks was looking to buy its first Black Apron reserve coffee, the pinnacle of its select micro-lot quality coffee. The coffee was so successful that Starbucks wanted to build its first Farmer Support Center for Africa in Rwanda, where agronomists provide free information to farmers about soil management, disease resistance, and other good practices. Due to the success of that work and the traceability efforts, I was hired as a contractor at Starbucks in 2008.

I went back and forth to Ethiopia for four years, and worked a total of seven years solely on traceability for Starbucks. My role in Ethiopia was introducing the country to the business, different stakeholders, and, more important, to others in the supply chain, showing them the value of data and content. There's a whole learning curve for most of the countries of origin about why we're doing this, what they get out of it, what we get out of it, how data and content and information are the new asset, and how to leverage it.

We worked on creating a value-based proposition within Starbucks that showed how data and content were important to the overall method. I encouraged them to go beyond a label on the bag, beyond certifications. All those are good sustainability checkmarks, things that help us remain ethical in our decisions. But they're verified by people too infrequently. It's an industry-wide concern. There's no way to double-check every grower every year. And because coffee is an agricultural product, season after season, people's circumstances and products change.

So my other value proposition was to make sure that we were using technology not only to back up ethical-sourcing claims with hard data and get more frequent verification checks, but also to pioneer the way coffee is grown and sustained. Since the first Yemenis moved coffee from Ethiopia to Saudi Arabia, coffee has been traded the same way: in gunnysacks on a boat. As far as we have advanced in how we drink and experience coffee every day, we're still stuck in the eleventh century at the supply chain. How do we advance that, considering the ubiquity of technology that we have today?

Traceability is interwoven with our efforts around sustainability. Over the years, many have questioned the coffee industry and how much investment goes into sustainability. I think it's become pretty evident in the last few years. The trends are slowly showing that people want to know more and more about where their goods come from, with a lot more detail. People are consuming content with commerce much more seamlessly thanks to information that comes with products.

Coffee saved my sanity. It saved my life. When I started working in coffee, I needed two things desperately. First, I needed to understand how to rid myself of the bitterness and anger I held for the perpetrators of the genocide in Rwanda. Second, I needed to know how to set up my war on poverty. I have become more and more convinced every day that I am on the right track. I believe what I started to be true. I have been witness and seen evidence. I am my own test case and I have more self-worth than can be destructed.

I'm still motivated by what my mother said to me. There have been many times that I've wanted to give up and just do something else. But her words kept me plowing on. Any time I take partners from Starbucks to Rwanda, they remind me to take some time and soak in a dose of pride in the achievements of the country, my people, our work there. They've seen images and heard stories of the past, and when they see what it is today, they're in disbelief.

I am proud to the extent that I've received what I was looking for in terms of validation. I've checked the selfish box. But I feel like there are still a lot of challenges and complexities ahead. I tell people that we're still playing catch-up. We sprinted quite fast to get where we are, but we're realizing that development isn't a 100-meter dash—it's a marathon. We're catching our breath and relacing our boots.